Church *Forward*

Alive Publishing Ltd

Church *Forward*
reflections on the renewal of the church

by
PETER HOCKEN

First published in 2007 by Alive Publishing Ltd
Graphic House, 124 City Road, Stoke on Trent ST4 2PH
Tel: +44 (0) 1782 745600 Fax: +44 (0) 1782 745500
www.biblealive.co.uk   e-mail: editor@biblealive.co.uk

Scripture texts used in this book are taken from the Revised Standard Version Bible with Apocryphal/Deutero-canonical Books. Copyrighted ©1965 and 1996. Used with permission.

©2007 Peter Hocken
British Library Catalogue-in-Publication Data. A catalogue record for this book is available
from the British Library.

All rights reserved. No part of this publication may be reproduced or transmitted in any form or by any means, electronic or mechanical, including photocopying, recording or any information storage and retrieval system, without either prior permission in writing from the publisher or a licence permitting restricted copying.

In the United Kingdom such licences are issued by the Publishers Licencing Society Ltd, 90 Tottenham Court Road, London W1P 9HE.
ISBN: 978 - 0 - 9540335 - 9 - 0

CONTENTS

Foreword		i
Introduction	Towards a Global Servant Church	vii

Part I

Prologue		3
Chapter 1	Blessed John XXIII	7
Chapter 2	Liturgy and Church	21
Chapter 3	Bible and Church	33
Chapter 4	The Dignity of the Human Person	45
Chapter 5	The Dignity of the Laity	55
Chapter 6	Christian Unity	65
Chapter 7	The Jewish People	77
Chapter 8	The Church as Communion	87

Part II

Prologue		101
Chapter 9	Evangelization	103
Chapter 10	Solidarity	117
Chapter 11	Repentance for the Sins of the Past	129
Chapter 12	New Ecclesial Movements	145
Chapter 13	The New Synthesis of John Paul II	165
Chapter 14	A New Ecumenism?	183

Part III

Prologue		197
Chapter 15	Believing the Faith	199
Chapter 16	Lived in Love	207
Chapter 17	Looking Forward in Joyful Hope	217
Glossary		223

FOREWORD

The idea for this book arose from the experience of teaching enthusiastic young Catholics about the renewal of the Catholic Church.[1] All those in the audience had been born well after the end of the Second Vatican Council. These young people are not budding theologian-scholars, but aspiring and trainee evangelists. They are not looking for academic lectures on Christology or ecclesiology, but they want teaching on Christ and the Church that will build their faith. They are seeking a vision for the future of the Church. For this, they need to understand how in the twentieth century the Holy Spirit has been renewing and reshaping the Church for her task in the twenty-first century. In this process, the Second Vatican Council has been central.

I am, in many ways, a Vatican II priest. I studied for the priesthood from 1958 to 1964. In my first year at seminary, Pope John XXIII announced the calling of the Council. During my theological studies, books like Hans Küng's *The Council and Reunion* made me aware of what was at stake in the Council and nourished my conciliar enthusiasm. When I was ordained in early 1964, the Council was at its mid-point, but with its essential direction evident and the Constitution on the Liturgy already completed. A weekly perusal of *Informations Catholiques Internationales*[2] and a daily listening to Vatican Radio, which slowly became more informative, kept me abreast of the unfolding events in Rome. As a result, I saw my priestly ministry in terms of helping the Catholic people to understand and receive the teachings and decisions of the Council.

At that time, I thought that the renewal of the Church would come about through the renewal of theology. That seemed to be what was happening at the Council. The Catholic theologians, whose works I was reading, were mostly *periti* at the Council, advising the bishops and making a major contribution. It was natural to assume that the post-conciliar renewal of the Church would come from the ongoing work of these theologians and their disciples. This vision of renewal would persist until my immersion in the charismatic movement in 1971. At this point, I became aware in a new way of the activity of the resurrected Jesus as Lord of the Church, and understood that renewal of the Church requires a listening and an obedience to the living Lord. I understood the Catholic charismatic renewal as an important element in the Lord's answer to Pope John's prayer for the Council: 'Renew in our day the wonders of Pentecost'.

From 1976 to 1996, I lived in the Mother of God Community near Washington, D.C., in the United States. My focus during these years was more on allowing the Holy Spirit to bring alive the whole of the biblical revelation than it was on the implementation of Vatican II. I was faced in a new way by the challenge of the Pentecostal movement and of the rise of new charismatic networks outside the world of historic Christianity. I had to learn about the working of the Holy Spirit. In time I became aware of the importance of the Jewish people in God's plan and for the unity of the Church. It was as though I had to be taken to the fringes of the Church before I could come back to the centre with a Holy Spirit-centred perspective.

In the meantime, there was John Paul II. By the time I returned from the USA to England in September 1996, it was clear that in all his teaching the Pope from Poland had been pursuing the deeper renewal of the Church, anchored in the foundational documents of Vatican II. Although I am aware of conflicting tendencies in the Catholic hierarchy, some very encouraging and some much less so, some favouring and some blocking ecumenical progress, I was never persuaded by what one might call the ultra-liberal thesis, that John Paul II was an old-fashioned Polish conservative trying to turn the clock back on Vatican II. For one thing, I have had more contact with Catholics in Poland. I discovered how untypical a Polish priest and bishop was Mgr Karol Wojtyla, later Pope John Paul II. I learned about his support for Fr Franciszek

Blachnicki and the Oasis movement.[3] I have met many Polish Catholic lay people, now in their forties and fifties, who caught the Council's vision but who have lacked official local encouragement in recent years. More importantly, I realized the depth of John Paul II's teaching and saw how it represents a remarkable new synthesis of Catholic teaching in the light of the conciliar renewal.

My appointment as bishop's chaplain (or secretary) to Bishop Leo McCartie of Northampton in June 1997 placed me squarely in the church institution, after years on the charismatic fringe. This was an important challenge, for it required a bringing together of the two perspectives, institutional and charismatic. But, whereas in the early 1970s I had largely seen the charismatic in terms of the Holy Spirit enlivening the whole Church, institution and all, now I saw the need to view the whole Church, including the institutional aspect, as being profoundly challenged by the Holy Spirit.

I found myself being brought back to Vatican II. When asked to give talks on the renewal of the Church, I was using the same data and calling upon the same memories from the 1960s; but I was coming at it from a new perspective. It is that perspective that I want to share in this book. It is the perspective in which the renewing purpose of the Holy Spirit is central. While Catholic presentations are regularly concerned to demonstrate the continuity with past tradition, this approach pays particular attention to the major breakthroughs and innovative elements. For it is these that make possible a profound renewal for the whole.

This is the fourth book of mine to be published by Alive Publishing. All three previous books have reflected on the work of the Holy Spirit in the Church. *Blazing the Trail* (2001) reflected on four major trends in the post-conciliar Church with the aim of helping Catholics to get a sense of the direction in which the Spirit is leading the Church. *God's Masterplan* (2003) examined the word 'mystery' in the New Testament so as to provide a biblical framework for understanding the work of the Holy Spirit in the Church today. *The Banquet of Life* (2004), an expansion of a series of articles on the dignity of the human person originally written for *Bible Alive*, reflected on different aspects of Catholic Social Teaching as they have developed in the teaching of the magisterium since the Council.

How does this book compare with its predecessors? It has the same focus on the work of the Holy Spirit as the earlier books. It has the same focus on the Holy Spirit's renewing work in the Church as *Blazing the Trail*. But it is more comprehensive and less selective. It devotes much more attention to the teaching and decisions of Vatican II. And it does more to bring the whole picture together: firstly through highlighting the theme of renewal and the unpacking of what this means; secondly, by the inclusion of more wide-ranging chapters, such as that on the new ecclesial movements (Chapter Twelve) and that on John Paul II's new synthesis of

Catholic teaching (Chapter Thirteen). In some ways, it brings together the spiritual renewal emphasis of *Blazing the Trail* and the social teaching focus of *The Banquet of Life*. Being more comprehensive in scope, the new book may help to fill out the understanding of those who have been helped by the earlier books. In some ways, it may complete a process of synthesis in the life of the author.

Peter Hocken
Vienna, January 2007

Notes

[1] This happened first within a course of ICPE (the International Catholic Programme for Evangelization) in Poland.

[2] Fr Yves Congar contributed a weekly column to ICI throughout the Council. These contributions appeared later as small books.

[3] See Chapter Thirteen.

INTRODUCTION
Towards a Global Servant Church

How different is the Catholic Church of the year 2000 from that of the year 1900? One of the most striking changes lies in the Church's increasingly global character. The Church of the year 1900 was a Europe-centred Church, ruled from a Rome dominated by clergy from the Italian peninsula and still smarting over the loss of the papal territories to the new republic of Italy. Out of sixty-one cardinals in January 1900, thirty-five were Italians. The heads of the various Vatican departments were almost all Italians.

The Pope was in effect 'the prisoner of the Vatican', unable to leave his small enclave around St Peter's basilica before 1929, when a treaty was signed between the republic of Italy and the newly formed state of Vatican City. But even then, the Popes did not travel. The first modern Pope to travel outside the Rome area was John XXIII, who visited the shrine of Loreto just before the opening of the Second Vatican Council in 1962. Paul VI was the first Pope of recent centuries to make pastoral journeys outside Italy, making a small number of mostly long but highly significant trips: to Jerusalem to meet Patriarch Athenagoras, to New York City to speak at the United Nations, to Medellin in Colombia, to Uganda, Sydney and Manila. But it was John Paul II who became the world-traveller. He made a hundred and four journeys outside Italy, visiting almost all countries where there is a Catholic community.

A hundred years ago, the Church in Europe was still in various ways tributary to political authorities, so that in the first papal election of the twentieth century the cardinal who gained the most votes on the first ballot was vetoed by the Emperor of Austria. Pius X who was then elected was probably not the first choice of the cardinals. In official church thinking the norm was the Catholic nation, in which the canonical authority of the Church is recognized by the State and laws are enacted in accordance with Catholic teaching. Protestant and non-Christian nations were considered as inferior and unsatisfactory situations, where the Church had to make the best of a 'bad job'.

The issues filling the Catholic mind in 1900 were still the issues that had preoccupied the Popes and the hierarchy throughout the nineteenth century. These were above all European battles, the legacy of the Church's power struggles with Josephism in the Habsburg Empire and with Gallicanism in France. The Church had fought a long battle to protect the authority of the Pope, and in the process had set herself against the political trends towards republicanism, democracy and freedom of speech. By 1900, the Church under Pope Leo XIII had begun to inch her way out of this cul de sac, mainly through his social encyclicals. But the prevailing habits of mind, especially of hierarchy and clergy, were suspicious of change, and this spirit was to affect the way in which Modernism was handled in the first decade of the new century.

While the missionary work of the Church had gained much ground, colonial ideas still prevailed, and the idea of developing an indigenous church leadership on the mission field had not gone far beyond the minds of a few visionary pioneers. The first African bishop was only ordained in 1939. The first cardinal from China was named in 1946, the first from India in 1953 and the first from black Africa in 1960. During the twentieth century, the Catholic population of Africa increased from just under two million in 1900 to 27 million in 1962 at the start of Vatican II. By 2000, this has grown to 130 million.[1]

The Influence of the Council

The Second Vatican Council itself played a major role in opening up the Catholic Church to a more global vision. The reformist majority at the Council came about through the missionary bishops from the Third World joining forces with the liturgical-theological reformers of northern Europe. The years of the Council coincided with the handing over of political control from the colonial powers to newly independent nations in Africa and Asia. The political changes made the missionary bishops acutely aware of the need for a truly indigenous Church in Africa, Asia and Latin America.

While at Vatican II many missionary bishops were themselves of European or North American origin, and less than half were native-born, it was the first ever Council where there was a clear missionary voice. Several missionary bishops made a significant contribution, as they urged much greater pastoral and liturgical flexibility in the Church's missionary work, and the need for a priestly formation that was not just imported from Europe.

With the Council's dogmatic teaching on the role of bishops in the Church came the decision to establish episcopal conferences in each nation with legal status in specified areas of pastoral concern. Thus the newly independent nations in Africa and Asia, as well as those in Latin America, acquired their own bishops' conferences, which was a further element in their progress towards adult status in the Church.

Introduction

The World Episcopate Today

At the turn of the twentieth century, there were approximately 1,500 Catholic bishops in the world. By the time of Vatican II, this had increased to 2,800. Both figures include auxiliaries. Today, the number is over 4,000 with 2,893 ecclesiastical territories (dioceses or equivalents) at the end of 2003. Of these some 600 are in Asia and approximately 460 in Africa.

The Internationalization of the Vatican

It was Pope Paul VI following the Council who recognized the need for an internationalizing of the Roman Curia and the Vatican's diplomatic service. Bishops throughout the world were encouraged to release suitable priests for service in the Vatican. Paul VI himself named several prelates from outside Italy, some from outside Europe, to head Vatican departments. He named a French cardinal, Jean Villot, as his Secretary of State, another French cardinal, Gabriel Garrone, to head the Congregation for Catholic Education, and an American, Cardinal John Wright, to the Congregation for the Clergy.

John Paul II and Benedict XVI have carried this internationalization further, so that among the prefects of the Roman Congregations, responsible under the Pope for the government of the Church, are cardinals from Nigeria, Syria,

Portugal, Poland, Slovenia, the USA, India and Brazil. Among the presidents of the Pontifical Councils are cardinals from Colombia, Germany, Mexico and France, as well as archbishops from Germany, Poland and the USA.[2] There has been a corresponding development in the diplomatic service of the Holy See. First of all, the number of countries having diplomatic relations with the Vatican has increased dramatically. The Vatican's diplomacy is no longer largely a matter of relating to the European powers and the Catholic nations. Secondly, whereas the vast majority of the Vatican's diplomats used to be Italians, today many nationalities are represented in the diplomatic service of the Holy See. The last two papal nuncios in Britain have both been from Spain. The papal diplomat murdered in Africa in December 2003 was an Irishman, Mgr Michael Courtney, the nuncio in Burundi.

Another clear sign of the move towards a global Church was evident in the interregnum between John Paul II and Benedict XVI. For the first time, there was a real possibility of a Pope from Africa, Asia and particularly Latin America. With the election of a German Pope, the epoch of an exclusively Italian papacy is clearly over, and the likelihood is that future conclaves will elect the most suitable candidate from whatever region of the globe he may come. The internationalization of the Catholic Church is continuing.

Introduction

The Style of Leadership

The style of the Catholic Church has also changed. In the shrine of the Immaculate Conception in Washington, D.C. there is an exhibit of the papal tiara that Pope Paul VI gave away for the benefit of the poor. The tiara is a three-tiered crown that symbolized the might of the papacy, the authority of Pope over kings, princes and peoples alike. The supreme moment in the installation of a new Pope had for centuries been his coronation with the golden tiara. With Paul VI and his successors, the tiara is gone. At the installation of a new Pope, he wears on his head the mitre of a bishop. Most recently, Benedict XVI has removed the triple tiara from the papal coat of arms, replacing it with the bishop's mitre.

Paul VI was the first Pope to insist that he was a bishop among his fellow bishops. When he entered the Council chamber for the first time as Pope, at the start of the Council's second session in 1963, he descended from the *sedia gestatoria* at the entrance to the basilica, and walked up the aisle between the banked rows of mitred bishops. Whereas the Pope had blessed the people outside, when he processed up the aisle, he simply saluted his fellow bishops. In his address, he said to the bishops: 'Greetings, brothers. It is in this way that the least one among you greets you, the Servant of the servants of God…'

Since that time, whenever the Pope gives his blessing at the end of any gathering, he invites his fellow bishops present to join him in giving the blessing together. Before the time of Vatican II, this never happened. The Pope was the head. Nobody else gave a blessing when the Pope was present. In fact, it had been forbidden for the bishops to wear the *mozzetta* when they were visiting Rome to show that in Rome only the Pope had authority. But Paul VI removed this prohibition soon after becoming Pope, again showing his respect for his fellow bishops. The vocation of Peter is not to dominate his brethren, but to confirm them (see Luke 22:32).

Other small details of papal apartness from others also began to disappear. Also gone is the tradition that the Pope had to eat in solitude. John Paul II regularly invited visitors to eat with him, and often held working breakfasts. When he flew to Israel in March, 2000, he invited his long-time Jewish friend, Jerzy Kluger, to travel with him.

Similarly, in the lives of the bishops there has been a parallel simplification. The age of the prince bishop is long past. Liturgical dress has been vastly simplified. Gone are special footwear and stockings. Gone is the *cappa magna,* a long train at one time carried by a member of the nobility. Many fussy and complicated details have been removed from episcopal liturgies, so that what is important can stand out more clearly. So, the cathedra, the seat in the cathedral from which the bishop presides, has to be prominent, for it represents the place of teaching, the principal ministry of the bishop according to Vatican II.

The style of life at Bishop's House has also become much simpler. Fifty years ago, the average bishop in Europe was cared for by a small community of nuns. Now there are fewer nuns, and probably only archbishops of major sees, who in any case have much greater responsibilities of hospitality, now have such a provision. A few bishops have sold their expensive properties. Cardinal Sean O'Malley in Boston, USA, and two bishops in England, Bishop Patrick O'Donoghue of Lancaster and Bishop Kieron Conry of Arundel and Brighton, have sold valuable mansions for more humble abodes. In fact, Bishop O'Donoghue has swapped the style of Bishop's House for a rotating pattern, whereby he spends time residing in each deanery of his diocese. This reflects the spread of a much more pastoral pattern of relationship between bishops and priests. Fifty years ago, young priests - then all curates - did not expect to have open and friendly conversations with their bishops, whereas today this would be a normal expectation.

During the Council, a number of bishops, especially from the French-speaking world, came together regularly to express their desire for a greater simplicity of lifestyle. These bishops found a ready ear in both the Popes of the Council. In fact, their initiatives had an influence on Paul VI's decision to give away his triple tiara to raise money for the poor.

The move towards being a servant Church closer to the poor has been shown most strikingly in the life of Mother Teresa of Calcutta and the Sisters of Charity. They always seek out places among the poor. Even when their home is not in a poor area, they seek to make the poor feel totally at home. In central Rome, alongside the Church and monastery of St Gregory the Great, the Sisters of Charity live in converted chicken huts, a location specifically chosen by Mother Teresa.

Another huge change in episcopal behaviour has resulted from the ecumenical movement. Fifty years ago, few Catholic bishops had any relationships with the leaders of other Christian Churches. Only a few bolder figures, like Cardinal Hinsley of Westminster, broke out of this pattern under the conditions of World War II. Today, it is normal for Catholic bishops to meet regularly with their Anglican and Free Church counterparts, and to be on Christian name terms.

The extraordinary attendance of church leaders and politicians at the funeral of John Paul II, including the unprecedented presence of the Patriarch of Constantinople and the Archbishop of Canterbury, shows a major change in the way the papal ministry is now being seen by those outside the Catholic Church. For the first time in many centuries, the Bishop of Rome is being looked to as the leader of the Christian world.

Introduction

The motivation for all these changes is to become more like Jesus, who came 'not to be served, but to serve' (Matt. 20:28). The motivation is to help people see Jesus when they look at the Church. This brings us into the topic of this book, the renewal of the Church. What does renewal mean? How does it happen? Where is it leading? These are the questions which this book seeks to answer.

Notes

[1] The Catholic statistics for the whole world are: 1900: 266,546,000 and 2000: 1,055,651,000 (taken from Documenting Global Statistics of World Mission, *International Bulletin of Missionary Research* 29/1 (Jan. 2005), p. 29).

[2] There is one Cardinal Prefect from Italy, and one Italian President of a Pontifical Council, along with an Italian Secretary of State.

PART I

Church *Forward*

PROLOGUE

In this reflection on renewal of Church, Part I will think about the contribution of Pope John XXIII and the Second Vatican Council. This reflection will not simply be a study of the Council's history and of the documents it produced. That has been done many times since the completion of the Council in 1965. My aim is to look back on the story and the achievements of the Council in the light of developments in the forty years since the Council (which will form the content of Part II) and in the light of the renewing work of the Holy Spirit.

It may be objected that such a reflection is too subjective. It could be just reading into the earlier history the particular emphases and enthusiasms of the author. To this objection, it can be said first that every reflection on past history inevitably contains a subjective dimension. But more importantly, I believe that it is the responsibility of all in the Church to reflect on this history seeking the light of the Holy Spirit for our understanding. If we believe that the Holy Spirit is the motor of renewal in the Church, then we will also believe that we need the light of the Holy Spirit to rightly read the 'signs of the times' and to understand the process of renewal that is under way. A Catholic attempt to read recent history in this way will, however, be marked by the recognition that every such attempt at scrutinizing the history has to be offered to the church community and leadership for their reflection and discernment.

In Part I, I look first at the crucial role played by Blessed John XXIII in the genesis of this ecclesial renewal (Chapter One). Then attention is given to the significance for renewal of the decision to begin with the Church's liturgy (Chapter Two). Then two foundational chapters highlight two key elements for renewal, which were much more revolutionary than has been generally realized or commonly admitted.[1] These are the role of the Word of God (Chapter Three) and the Dignity of the Human Person (Chapter Four). I see these two elements as driving forward the whole dynamic of renewal in the Church. The remaining chapters in Part I then examine particular areas of application: the Laity (Chapter Five), Christian Unity (Chapter Six), the Jewish People (Chapter Seven), and the understanding of Church as communion (Chapter Eight).

Notes

[1] While following the traditional Roman practice of emphasizing continuity with the past, John Paul II shows himself to be aware of the radical character of the Council's decisions: 'Entrusting myself fully to the Spirit of truth,

therefore, I am entering into the rich inheritance of the recent pontificates. This inheritance has struck deep roots in the awareness of the Church in an utterly new way, quite unknown previously, thanks to the Second Vatican Council'. (*Redemptor hominis,* para. 3).

Church *Forward*

CHAPTER ONE
Blessed John XXIII

The pontificate of John XXIII was a turning-point for the renewal of the Church. Pope John's most significant contribution came from who he was, rather than from any brilliant idea or master-plan. Above all, it came from his trust in God, the providence of the Father, the love of Christ and the guidance of the Holy Spirit.

The turning-point for the Catholic Church of the twentieth century came on 28 October, 1958. On this day an elderly Italian cardinal, only a month short of his seventy-seventh birthday, was elected Pope. His election was a surprise, even a shock, as few Catholics outside Italy knew anything about the Cardinal Patriarch of Venice, Angelo Giuseppe Roncalli, except in France, where he had served as papal nuncio from 1945 to 1953. Although Cardinal Roncalli would only be Pope for a short four and a half years, his was a papacy of constant surprises. The first surprise was his choice of name. In the ritual of a papal election, two questions are put to the newly elected Bishop of Rome. The first: 'Do you accept?' The second: 'What name will you be called?' Roncalli answered: 'Vocabor Johannes.' 'I will be called John.'

The name John had not been used since an anti-Pope had taken the name of John XXIII about 550 years before. The last authentic Pope John, known as John XXII, had been one of the longer-reigning Popes in the Middle Ages, holding office from 1316 to 1334. No other Pope since the Reformation had reached back to choose a name unused for such a long time. Why John? It seems that the new Pope had three Johns in mind: his own father Giovanni, St John the Baptist and St John the Apostle, the disciple whom the Lord loved.

The contrast with his predecessor, Pope Pius XII, was stark: the image of the portly, gregarious and jolly John XXIII was totally different from that of the aristocratic, ascetic and dignified Pius XII. Stories quickly circulated of the new Pope's jokes, enough later to fill a whole book. Pius XII had never been known to tell a joke.

Did the cardinals who elected their brother from Venice have any idea of the revolution their decision would unleash? As a group almost certainly not, though his old friend Cardinal Feltin of Paris may have had some inkling. The press immediately dubbed John a 'caretaker Pope', chosen to tide things over for a short interim reign before a candidate of more obvious weight and stature could be chosen. Most of the cardinal electors probably saw Roncalli as a genuinely good man of deep piety and with the heart of a pastor. This reading of the papal election of 1958 is highly plausible, as the 'obvious candidate' to succeed Pius XII was Archbishop Giovanni Battista Montini of Milan. But there was a major obstacle to Montini's election. Pius XII had never made him a cardinal. John XXIII would immediately make Montini a cardinal, preparing the way for his election as Pope Paul VI in 1963.

But the next four and a half years were going to be far from the quiet pastoral interlude envisioned. John XXIII would change the face of the Catholic Church. He was not a reformer, and he would not change the face of the Church by major decisions from on high. The secret of John XXIII was his trust in the Holy Spirit. Just before the cardinals entered the conclave, Cardinal Roncalli had written to the Bishop of Bergamo, his home diocese: 'my soul finds comfort in the confidence that a new Pentecost can blow through the Church.' Throughout his long service of God and the Church, he had learned to trust in the Holy Spirit. His years as apostolic delegate in Bulgaria and Turkey had showed him the place of the Holy Spirit in the life of the Orthodox Church. John XXIII did not really have a plan, but he did have a vision. His vision was for a 'new Pentecost', and the instrument would be a general Council of the Church. But he did not have a plan for the Council. For that, he trusted the Holy Spirit, and understood that a renewal of the Church required constant trust in the Holy Spirit. He unlocked the door through which others would walk.

Pope John, as everyone called him, breathed a different spirit. Sometimes his talks and sermons were not very inspiring, but what came through was the simplicity of his faith and the warmth of his humanity. He was a man full of faith and love. Deep in his heart, in his love for the Lord and for the Church, he knew the need for renewal, and he knew that renewal had to be the work of the Holy Spirit. When he became Pope, he did not act as a master politician, building up a coalition, trying to win over different factions to his ideas. It was the way Pope John lived rather than by big decisions that he set the tone for the Council.

With his confidence in the Holy Spirit, John XXIII had learned to trust in the goodness of God. While he was in no way a rebellious, angry spirit, he was never comfortable with the reigning spirit of suspicion that encouraged denunciation and worked by condemnation. These negative mentalities had originated in the shock of the Reformation, but they had become more entrenched with the assaults of secularism and unbelief in the nineteenth century. The more the Church was attacked, the more the defences went up. The response of the Church to 'modernism' under Pius X and to Communism under Pius XI and Pius XII continued firmly in this uncompromising separation and opposition. John XXIII felt profoundly uncomfortable with the fortress-Church. Already in Venice, he had manifested a different spirit. In 1957, the

Italian Socialist party had held its annual congress in Venice. The church authorities traditionally kept their distance from such events, regarding them as the camp of the enemy. Cardinal Roncalli, however, welcomed the Socialist party to Venice and prayed publicly that the congress might help bridge the gap between Catholic and secular culture. Officially there was silence from the Vatican, but privately it was said that the Patriarch was rebuked for his naivety. Likewise Cardinal Roncalli adopted a quite different attitude to the famous Biennale art festival held in Venice every other year. His predecessors had denounced the show as immoral, but Cardinal Roncalli opened the hall of the patriarchal palace to the artists. He had learned always to look first for the qualities in 'the others' and not first for their defects. He looked first to the person, not to what was wrong with their theology or their politics.

It was this spirit of trusting openness that Pope John brought to the Vatican. Many there thought he was just naïve, a nice 'old boy' who wasn't in touch with reality. He had not developed a theology of dialogue, but he was already living the dialogue that his successor Paul VI was to commend as 'the way of the Church'. He quickly ended the tradition of four centuries that the Pope took his meals alone. He asked his chauffeur to drive him to the poor areas of Rome, where he would emerge from his limousine and talk to people on the streets. He chatted with workmen in the Vatican. But the first public episode that made headlines around the world was Pope John's visit to the Regina Coeli prison on Christmas Day, 1958. Here Pope John struck an instant rapport with the prisoners. Whereas a mystique of the papacy had elevated Popes above the ordinary run of humanity, Papa Giovanni emphasized what he had in common with everyone. With the prisoners he shared how one of his brothers had been caught poaching, and how an uncle had been sent to prison. These things happen to poor people, he said. Such simplicity, such honesty, was all astounding for those accustomed to the solemn rituals of Vatican protocol.

For those who knew Pope John, it was clear that his openness would lead to a different approach to other Christians. When he was elected Pope, an old friend of many years was bed-ridden in a Belgian monastery. Dom Lambert Beauduin had been a founder-figure in both the liturgical and the ecumenical movements within the Catholic Church. Because Beauduin's vision for Christian unity was far ahead of the church authorities of his day, he was exiled from his monastery for nearly twenty years. But he had remained a friend of Mgr Roncalli, whose experience in Bulgaria and Turkey had deepened his heart for Christian unity and for reconciliation between the Catholic and Orthodox Churches. For Beauduin, the election of John XXIII was like the presentation of the infant Jesus for Simeon; it was a confirmation of the longings of decades and a glimpse of a more glorious future before he died.

In fact, the world did not have to wait long for the new Pope to sound a new note about Christian unity. In his first broadcast on Vatican radio the day after his election, Pope John spoke of the Lord's prayer 'that all may be one'. The rest of the Christian world began to sense a different spirit in this Pope. When, on 25 January 1959, he announced the calling of an 'Ecumenical Council', some not surprisingly thought this meant a Council for the restoration of unity. While this official Catholic language has no direct connection with the movement towards Christian unity, Pope John did see a connection between Christian unity and his Council, which he told the cardinals would be a 'friendly and renewed invitation to our brothers of the separated Christian Churches to share with us in this banquet of grace'.

Not surprisingly, leaders of other Christian Churches began to express an interest in coming to Rome and meeting the Pope. One of the first to come was the Archbishop of Canterbury, Dr Geoffrey Fisher, in 1960, the first official visit of an Archbishop of Canterbury to a Pope since the Reformation. Such an occasion caused protocol headaches in the Vatican, because there was no tradition for handling such visitors. Pope John realized that in the traditional Roman set-up there was no address to which other church leaders could refer. So he established a new office to handle relations with other Christians. The so-named Secretariat for Promoting Christian Unity was formed in 1960 under the leadership of a newly named cardinal, the German Jesuit,

Augustin Bea, a biblical scholar and a former confessor of Pius XII. Bea was an astute choice for this important new responsibility. As a German biblical scholar, he was familiar with Protestant biblical scholarship. As former confessor to Pius XII, he had respect in Rome. The same age as the Pope, Bea could hardly be dismissed as a dangerous radical.

It soon became clear that Pope John was serious in his approach towards other Christians. His secretariat began to send out invitations to the Orthodox and Protestant Churches and communities for them to send official observers to the Council. It is hard for us now to realize what a shock this decision was to many in the Catholic hierarchy and in the Vatican. Pope John was calling them 'separated brethren', but in the theological textbooks they had been called *adversarii*, opponents designated by their errors, whose books Catholics were not allowed to read. Now Protestant and Orthodox leaders and theologians were to be admitted to the Council debates, to be handed copies of confidential draft documents, and to be asked for their opinions. Well before the Council's Decree on Ecumenism came out in 1964, the bishops had the new experience of making friends with the non-Catholic observers during the coffee breaks in St Peter's and at other social events in Rome.

A new attitude to the Jewish people soon became apparent. One of the first signs of a new attitude to the Jews came in John XXIII's first Holy Week as Pope. He ordered the removal from the Good Friday liturgy of words deeply offensive to the Jewish people.[1] Also much advertised was the Pope's meeting with a large group of American Jews in October 1960. They came to Rome to thank the Holy Father for his efforts in Turkey for the Jewish people during the Nazi persecution, which led to some thousands being saved. Pope John greeted his Jewish visitors with the words, 'Son io, Giuseppe, il fratello vostro'. 'I am Joseph, your brother'.

The openness of Pope John to unbelievers was also remarkable. He believed that the gospel of Christ is stronger and more infectious than other philosophies. Secret overtures to the Soviet leader, Nikita Khrushchev, led to his sending the Pope a greeting on his eightieth birthday in November 1961. John XXIII responded: 'The wide-ranging nature of the birthday greetings we have received permits us to embrace, in a single gesture of affection, the beloved children of the Catholic Church and the entire human family.'

John XXIII's trust in the Holy Spirit was seen especially in his handling of the Council. He set the tone in his opening speech on 11 October, 1962. He spoke of 'the dignity of the human person' as a 'supreme value'. He expressed his disagreement with the 'prophets of doom' in the Church, who are convinced that the world is going from bad to worse. The Pope astonished many by rejoicing in the freedom of the Church from the State, taking a quite different line to the Popes of the nineteenth century. 'The princes of this world, in effect, often presented themselves as loyal protectors of the Church, but, most often, this was a danger for the spiritual, for the princes acted as politicians, with their own interests, which was dangerous. ... It is with great hope and great reassurance that we see the Church today finally set free from so many obstacles.' Finally, he indicated that the purpose of the Council was not just to reiterate old truths in old language, but 'the authentic teaching will be set forth following the methods of research and of presentation used in modern thought.' The Holy Father then made a bold distinction: 'The substance of the ancient teaching contained in the deposit of faith is one thing, the formulation in which it is clothed is another.'

On the first working day of the Council, those waiting outside St Peter's had a big surprise. The bishops were on their way back to their lodgings by mid-morning. The business was due to begin with the election of the commissions of bishops that would work on the Council's documents. The problem was that most of the bishops did not know the bishops from other nations, and the only list provided would re-appoint the bishops who had served on the preparatory commissions over the previous two years. So at the outset, Cardinal Achille Liénart, the senior French cardinal, proposed an adjournment of the Council so that the bishops could get to know each other and draw up lists of suitable candidates. This proposal was immediately seconded by the senior German cardinal, Josef Frings of Cologne. Both speeches were greeted with loud applause.

The presiding cardinal then declared the session closed with a week to prepare for the election of the commission members. The signs were that John XXIII was delighted that the Council assembly had taken this initiative and had acted as a body.

Only on one occasion did Pope John intervene during the first session of the Council. This followed a vote on the draft schema *De fontibus revelationis* (The Sources of Revelation). This subject produced the most impassioned debate of the first session, for it brought face to face the defenders of the dogmatic theology of the Counter-Reformation and the proponents of a more patristic, historically conscious and ecumenically open approach. We can say this was a debate between those who understood tradition as the textbook teaching of the last four hundred years and those who understood tradition as embracing the whole life and history of the Church through nearly two thousand years. When the question was asked: 'Do you approve of this schema being sent back for revision?', the vote for revision was 1,368 and the vote against 822. However, since the rules of the Council required a two-thirds majority, the majority was not a sufficient percentage to send back the document for revision. This produced a somewhat absurd situation, in which the procedure required the retention of a document that over 60 per cent of the bishops regarded as unsatisfactory. At this point Pope John intervened to accept a proposal, already made by a few bishops, that the document be redrafted by a mixed commission drawn from two commissions, the theological and the ecumenical. In other words, the Pope intervened to solve a procedural impasse, not to impose his own preference.

In John XXIII we can see the beginnings of a different papacy: a papacy that trusts the bishops; a papacy that is not only leading the Catholic Church, but acting as the servant-leader of the Christian world; a papacy that is not primarily defending the Church against the world, but which serves the whole of humanity by sifting the good from the bad. This latter aspect was especially visible in Pope John's final testament, the encyclical letter *Pacem in terris,* issued at Easter 1963, just two months before his death. Papal encyclicals are traditionally addressed to the bishops of the world; but here, for the first time, an encyclical letter was addressed to 'all people of good will'. Hidden in the midst of this encyclical are little hints of the revolution to come. 'A man who has fallen into error does not cease to be a man. He never forfeits his personal dignity; and that is something that must always be taken into account' (para. 158). This was a direct refutation of the position that 'error has no rights', the theology of Cardinal Ottaviani, the Prefect of the Holy Office, and the theology that had controlled Vatican policy for so long.

The extraordinary impact of 'good Pope John' was shown in the final hours of his life and in the response to the news of his death. At Pentecost 1963, the world knew that the

Pope was dying. On Pentecost Monday, 3 June, a huge crowd gathered in St Peter's Square to pray for the dying Pope. As the evening Mass came to an end, John XXIII breathed his last. The press coverage of the Pope's final hours and of his death was extraordinary, making the top headlines in largely Protestant countries as well as in Catholic. In some way, the world knew better than the Church, or the ordinary faithful knew better than the clergy, how different was John XXIII and how he had launched the Catholic Church on a new road whose route and contours no-one could yet fathom.

Notes

[1] The word deleted, *perfidis*, which had originally simply meant "non-believing", had come to connote perfidy and betrayal, and so to have a strongly emotive and negative meaning.

Church *Forward*

CHAPTER TWO
Liturgy and Church

A renewal of the Church is impossible without renewal of the Church's worship. Communal worship expresses the relationship of a faith community to the God it worships. Christian worship expresses the foundation of the Church in the mystery of the death and resurrection of Jesus Christ. Authentic renewal of the Church requires a revitalized relationship with God in Christ for each expression of Church. All other dimensions of Church renewal depend on this, the renewal of our relationship with the triune God we worship.

The Council of renewal began with the liturgy. The renewal of the liturgy was the first subject to be debated, and the Constitution on the Liturgy (*Sacrosanctum concilium*) was the first document to be completed. This choice was truly providential because the liturgy reveals the Church in her deepest reality. The Church expresses her nature most fully in her corporate worship of the one God, Father, Son and Holy Spirit. The renewal of the liturgy directly promotes the renewal of the Church. As a result, *Sacrosanctum concilium* contains several key elements for the renewal of the theology of the Church that will be more fully developed in the Constitution on the Church (*Lumen gentium*).

Trinitarian Liturgy and Trinitarian Church

The Church is not primarily a religious institution, but a people gathered in Christ by the Holy Spirit to worship the Father. This vision is expressed at the start of Eucharistic Prayer no. III: 'Father, you are holy indeed, and all creation rightly gives you praise. All life, all holiness comes from you through your Son, Jesus Christ our Lord, by the working of the Holy Spirit.' This prayer reaches its climactic conclusion in the great doxology, used in every eucharistic prayer in the Roman rite: 'Through him [Christ], with him, in him, in the unity of the Holy Spirit, all glory and honour is yours, Almighty Father, for ever and ever. Amen.'

The Church has a Trinitarian shape, because the Church is formed by the self-giving love of the Trinitarian God. The renewal of the Church recalls us to this Trinitarian pattern. We are not just worshipping a God out there, or a God inside us. Through the Holy Spirit, poured out by the crucified and risen Lord Jesus, we are made into sons and daughters of the Father in the image of his Son. In the liturgy, we are drawn into this Trinitarian movement, out from the Father through the Spirit and then back from the Son through the Spirit to the Father. The Spirit leads Jesus out from the Father to his total self-emptying in his passion and death, and then raises him to glory at the right hand of the Father. Through the risen Christ, the Holy Spirit is poured out to draw us into Christ, into his death and resurrection, so that we may be conformed to him and restored to the Father. The Church is this communion of life in the crucified and risen Christ through the Holy Spirit.

In the liturgy, and especially in the Eucharist, we are being formed into the Church. So, the Constitution on the Liturgy will state: 'every liturgical celebration, because it is an action of Christ the Priest and of his Body, which is the Church, is a sacred action surpassing all others' (para. 7). The Church's liturgy has a unique character that no other prayers possess, even those blessed and encouraged by church authority. It is uniquely the worship of Jesus Christ, the Head, and of his Body, the Church. In the worship of the liturgy, the Church is being drawn into the action of Jesus Christ within the Trinity, and in this way becomes more conformed to her Lord within the unique communion of the Triune Godhead.

In this way the Constitution on the Liturgy was preparing the way for the Constitution on the Church, which in its opening paragraphs expresses this Trinitarian pattern with a paragraph on the Father (LG, para. 2), a paragraph on the Son (LG, para. 3) and a paragraph on the Holy Spirit (LG, para. 4). The Church comes forth from the Trinity, is shaped into the pattern of the Trinity, manifests the Trinity to the world and gives glory to the Trinity. This pattern will be followed later in the *Catechism of the Catholic Church*. The Church is the People of God (paras. 781-786), the Body of Christ (paras. 787-796) and the Temple of the Holy Spirit (paras. 797-801).[1]

An important lesson follows. We cannot talk rightly about the liturgy and we cannot talk rightly about the Church without speaking of Father, Son and Holy Spirit. When we speak about liturgy and Church without reference to Father, Son and Holy Spirit, we diminish that of which we speak. We reduce and distort the most personal and profound reality into a 'thing': we reduce the liturgy to an activity or a rite. We reduce the Church to an institution, or to a religious society.

Formed by the Word of God

It is significant that the Council first discussed the Bible in the context of the Church's worship. There is a natural sequence from Word to Faith to Worship. The place of the Word in the liturgy leads naturally into the role of the Word of God in the Church. Even when the liturgy was in a language that few people understood, there was always a liturgy of the Word, with readings from the Sacred Scriptures. It was a reminder of the unique role of the Bible as the inspired Word of God, a role that cannot be played by any other literature, however worthy and spiritually inspiring.

As the next chapter will look at the role of the Bible in the whole life of the Church, this section is limited to the restored role of the Scriptures in the liturgy, while noting its importance for every aspect of church life. The bishops state that 'Sacred scripture is of the greatest importance in the celebration of the liturgy' (SC, para. 24). This paragraph then shows how the Bible has shaped the liturgy: it is read in the readings, and sung in the psalms; it has inspired and influenced the prayers, the collects and the hymns; and it gives meaning to the liturgical signs and actions. This paragraph ends by saying in rather flowery language that the renewal of the liturgy is impossible without a deep love for the Scriptures. The text speaks of a 'sweet and living love' that echoes the language of St Bernard of Clairvaux. It is not just academic knowledge of the Bible that is needed, but a warm, heartfelt love that is one with our love for Jesus and our love for God.

With its teaching on the Word of God, the Constitution on the Liturgy presented a unified vision of Catholic worship in which there is no 'gap' or 'opposition' between Word and sacrament. 'The two parts, which in a sense go to make up the Mass,...the liturgy of the word and the eucharistic liturgy, are so closely connected with each other that they form but one single act of worship' (para. 56). The Word of God is an essential element in the eucharistic action. It is not just a preamble to 'the real thing' in the sacraments. The Catechism develops this understanding more explicitly: 'In the Liturgy of the Word the Holy Spirit "recalls" to the assembly all that Christ has done for us' (para. 1103). This memorial in the liturgy of the Word then leads on to the memorial in the eucharistic action: 'Christian liturgy not only recalls the events that saved us but actualizes them, makes them present' (para. 1104).

To aid the acquisition of this loving knowledge of the Bible, the Council decided in its chapter on the Eucharist that: (1) a bigger selection of biblical texts would be read at Mass; (2) the homily preached at Mass should 'expound' the biblical texts; (3) the homily is an integral part of the liturgy (not an interruption) and should not be omitted on Sundays or holidays of obligation without a serious reason (SC, paras. 51-52). This wording implies that homilies should also be preached at Mass on other occasions.

Active Participation

The schema on the liturgy also prepared the way for the Constitution on the Church in its presentation of the role of the laity. The phrase 'active participation' sums up the vision of the Council. It is the duty of the pastors 'to ensure that the faithful take part [in the liturgy] fully aware of what they are doing, actively engaged in the rite and enriched by it' (SC, para. 11). 'To promote active participation, the people should be encouraged to take part by means of acclamations, responses, psalms, antiphons, hymns, as well as by actions, gestures and bodily attitudes' (SC, para. 30). Participation is not primarily getting people to sing, make responses and join in the offertory procession, but for all to become active agents (body, mind, voice, spirit) in the celebratory worship of the one People of God. 'The Church...earnestly desires that Christ's faithful, when present at this mystery of faith, should not be there as strangers or silent spectators' (SC, para. 48). This teaching represents a revolution from the dominant piety of the Counter-Reformation with the priest 'saying Mass' at which the people 'assist' or 'attend'. Now the liturgy is 'celebration' by the whole people of God, among whom particular members exercise specific ministries.

Here we see a new dynamic vision for the Catholic people. Active participation in the liturgy, active participation in the Church. No second-class membership, no spectators, no passivity. This active role of the laity will be developed in a later chapter.[2]

Ministry in the Church

Along with a new vision for the people goes a new vision of ministry. Here too the Constitution on the Liturgy prepared the way for the Constitution on the Church. The multiplicity of roles in the Church is first indicated in the teaching on the many forms of the Lord's presence in the liturgy, that is, in the gathered Church. 'To accomplish so great a work Christ is always present in his Church, especially in her liturgical celebrations. He is present in the sacrifice of the Mass not only in the person of his minister,...but especially in the eucharistic species. By his power he is present in the sacraments... He is present in his word...Lastly he is present when the Church prays and sings' (para. 7).

In the priest who presides at the Eucharist, there is a distinctive form of the presence of Christ. This presence is to be understood in relation to the other forms of presence, not as standing on its own. This presence in the ministering priest is not to be understood as rendering the laity passive. Within the vision of the active participation of all the laity, there are various liturgical services rendered by lay people: the Constitution mentions servers, readers, commentators, and members of the choir' (SC, para. 29).[3]

But in the liturgy as a celebration of the Church, not legally but existentially, there is a forming of community. The essentially collaborative character of Christian ministry is demonstrated. No ministry stands isolated on its own. Each ministry takes its place within the ministry of the whole body: 'liturgical services pertain to the whole Body of the Church' (SC, para. 26). Priests are not lone rangers, but take their place in the body of priests around their bishop. Bishops are not just local church officials, but are pastors of local churches and belong to the body of bishops (later in LG called the 'college' of bishops) united around the Bishop of Rome, the successor of Peter. This essentially collaborative and corporate vision of ordained ministry was foreshadowed in the Constitution on the Liturgy by the restoration of concelebration in the Eucharist 'whereby the unity of the priesthood is appropriately manifested' (SC, para. 57. 1).

The restoration of concelebration makes possible once again the visible liturgical sign of the unity of the Church, described in *Sacrosanctum concilium*, paragraph 41: 'the principal manifestation of the Church consists in the full, active participation of all God's holy people in the same liturgical celebrations, especially in the same Eucharist, in one prayer, at one altar, at which the bishop presides, surrounded by his college of priests and by his ministers.' It is this sacramental vision of the bishop's ministry that prepares the way for the teaching of *Lumen gentium* on the sacramental character of episcopal ordination as the fullness of the sacrament of orders.

Come, Lord Jesus!

Treating the liturgy first also demonstrated the link between the heavenly and the earthly Church and the way in which the Church is oriented to and longs for the coming of the Lord in glory. This dimension had little or no place in the Counter-Reformation presentations of the Church, which were focused on defending her earthly powers and privileges.

The Constitution on the Liturgy teaches: 'In the earthly liturgy we take part in a foretaste of that heavenly liturgy which is celebrated in the Holy City of Jerusalem toward which we journey as pilgrims, where Christ is sitting at the right hand of God, Minister of the sanctuary and of the true tabernacle' (para. 8). This aspect of the life of the Church as the communion of saints is expressed in every Mass at the end of the Preface and in the Sanctus that follows: 'And so, with all the choirs of angels in heaven we proclaim your glory and join in their unending hymn of praise: Holy, holy, holy Lord, God of power and might, heaven and earth are full of your glory. Hosanna in the highest. Blessed is he who comes in the name of the Lord. Hosanna in the highest.'[4]

The affirmation of the union between the company of heaven and the Church on earth in their worship of the all-holy God leads into a proclamation of the coming of the Lord Jesus. So paragraph 8 continues: 'With all the warriors of the heavenly army we sing a hymn of glory to the Lord; venerating the memory of the saints, we hope for some part and fellowship with them; we eagerly await the Saviour, Our Lord Jesus Christ, until he our life shall appear and we too will appear with him in glory.'

In this way, the Holy Spirit prepared the bishops for the inclusion in *Lumen gentium* of a chapter on 'The Pilgrim Church',[5] which treats of the relationship between the Church militant on earth and the Church in glory. It will emphasize what the liturgy clearly expresses, that the Church is moving towards a goal, the total realization of God's eternal plan in Christ. This aspect of the liturgy would be further expressed in the Catechism: 'Since the apostolic age the liturgy has been drawn toward its goal by the Spirit's groaning in the Church: "Marana tha!" The liturgy thus shares in Jesus' desire: "I have earnestly desired to eat this Passover with you ... until it is fulfilled in the kingdom of God"' (para. 1130).[6]

Notes

[1] Later in Part II of the Catechism on the Liturgy (called 'The Celebration of the Christian Mystery'), the first article is entitled 'The Liturgy - Work of the Holy Trinity', with three sections: 'The Father - Source and Goal of the Liturgy' (paras. 1077-1083); 'Christ's Work in the Liturgy' (paras. 1084-1090) and 'The Holy Spirit and the Church in the Liturgy' (paras. 1091-1109).

[2] Chapter Five.

[3] Deacons are not mentioned in the Constitution, as the decision to restore the permanent diaconate was only taken after its promulgation.

[4] From Weekday Preface I.

[5] Chapter Seven.

[6] See also *Catechism of the Catholic Church,* paras. 1090, 1107 and 1403.

Church *Forward*

CHAPTER THREE

Bible and Church

There can be no authentic renewal of the Church without a return to the biblical sources. The Scriptures 'are able to instruct you for salvation through faith in Christ Jesus' (2 Tim. 3:15). The Word of God is central to the renewal of the liturgy and central to the whole life of faith. Access to the Bible is for all the faithful.

Vatican II has been a watershed for the Catholic Church. One major element is the return to the sources, and in particular to the Bible. It would be no exaggeration to say that before Vatican II the Catholic Church had no theology of the Word. But now, as a theology of the Word is beginning to develop, there is an increasing recognition of the centrality of the Word of God for Catholic life.

The seeds planted by the Second Vatican Council are beginning to show their fruit, as will be illustrated in later chapters.[1] Here it is important to identify the seeds, and to understand their importance for the future renewal of the Church. The last chapter outlined the contribution of the Constitution on the Liturgy concerning the Bible. The liturgy of the Word is an integral element in Catholic liturgy. More of the Bible is to be read at Mass, both on Sundays and on weekdays. The homily is to relate the Scriptures to contemporary life. The Bible provides the basis and the meaning for the sacramental signs. The formal theological teaching on the Bible was to follow in the Dogmatic Constitution on Divine Revelation, *Dei verbum*.

Divine Revelation

After the debate on the liturgy in the Council's first session, two days were given to a draft document on 'The Sources of Revelation' (*De fontibus revelationis*). It was soon clear that the majority of the bishops were unhappy with any teaching presenting the Bible and Tradition as two separate sources of divine revelation. Such a formulation, that had characterized the manuals of theology in use before the Council, removes Tradition from the controlling role of Scripture and obscures the personal character of revelation that finds its full expression in the person of Jesus. A new approach was needed. The new document that resulted was entitled 'On

Divine Revelation' (*Dei verbum*) and was centred on the concept of 'The Word of God'.

The Council's schematic teaching on the Word of God is rich, but not easy to grasp. On the one hand, the bishops seek to be faithful to the Catholic tradition which has always recognized an element of duality in the roles of Scripture and Tradition. The two cannot be reduced to one. The Church has been a living community of faith from the Day of Pentecost, preaching the message of Jesus and enacting his commands before the New Testament came to be written and to be recognized as canonical Scripture. But, on the other hand, the recognition of the Canon of Sacred Scripture, inspired by the Holy Spirit, makes the Bible a privileged source, a unique written witness to divine revelation. So the bishops sought to emphasize the unity and coherence of the whole, to ensure that Scripture and Tradition are understood in their relationship to each other.

Thus, in the teaching of the Council and, later, of the Catechism, the Word of God is expressed both in Scripture and in Tradition. 'Sacred Scripture is the speech of God as it is put down in writing under the breath of the Holy Spirit. And Tradition transmits in its entirety the Word of God which has been entrusted to the apostles by Christ the Lord and the Holy Spirit' (DV, para. 9). Here it is clear that 'Tradition' means not just what was done and believed in previous generations, but the whole reality of the Church (teaching, witness, worship, mission) as it was founded by the Lord and enlivened by the Holy Spirit.

The Church is not founded on the Bible, but on the apostles and their witness to Jesus. However, the Bible is the privileged expression of this witness, because it is the witness inspired by the Holy Spirit. That is to say, the Scriptures contain what God wanted to be put in writing for the sake of the Church. As *Dei verbum* later states: 'since they are inspired by God and committed to writing once and for all time, they present God's Word in an unalterable form, and they make the voice of the Holy Spirit sound again and again in the words of the prophets and apostles' (para. 21).

In this Catholic vision, Scripture and Tradition belong together. 'Sacred Tradition and sacred Scripture make up a single sacred deposit of the Word of God, which is entrusted to the Church' (DV, para. 10). They cannot be separated. It is impossible to have Scripture without Tradition: first, because the formation of the Scriptures happened as part of the development of the Church, i.e., as part of Tradition; second, because we cannot receive Scripture without receiving an interpretation of the Scriptures (e.g., the whole heritage of the Creeds), and that is part of Tradition. However, it is also impossible to have Tradition without the Scriptures. The Tradition, which is both what is transmitted and the process of transmission, hands on what is in the Scriptures. Even those doctrines of the Church that may be regarded as not demonstrable from the Bible are impossible to understand without the Scriptures.[2]

But while the Council manifests this effort at 'balancing', by distinguishing Scripture and Tradition and then holding them together in unity, there is another trend visible in the Council documents. This trend is to exalt Scripture to a higher place, and to insist on its unique irreplaceable role in the Church and in her life. Here we can recognize that the Holy Spirit is highlighting the Scriptures as a key element in the renewal of the Church. Instead of Scripture just being there somewhere in the midst of Tradition, Scripture is being raised up within the Church. 'In Sacred Scripture, the Church constantly finds her nourishment and her strength, for she welcomes it not as a human word, "but as what it really is, the word of God"' (CCC, para. 104).

This special place of the Scriptures, now recognized in a new way, has many practical implications. First, 'Access to sacred Scripture ought to be open wide to the Christian faithful' (DV, para. 22). Second, the Scriptures provide food for every Christian, so the Church 'strives to reach day by day a more profound understanding of the sacred Scriptures, in order to provide her children with food from the divine words' (DV, para. 23). Third, all theological study has to be rooted in the Scriptures. 'Therefore, the "study of the sacred page" should be the very soul of sacred theology' (DV, para. 24).

These principles are foundational for the renewal of the Church. No longer is Bible-reading just to be the hallmark of the Protestant Christian. No longer can we separate the food of the Eucharist from the food of the Word, the table of 'God's Word' from the table of 'Christ's Body'.[3]   No longer can Scripture be a Cinderella subject in Catholic studies. No longer can we have a theology that makes occasional references to the Scriptures to back up an exposition that is really drawn from other sources.

The Uniqueness of the Scriptures and the Uniqueness of Christ

A lifting up of the Scriptures is a lifting up of Jesus Christ. The centrality of the Bible in Christian life is directly connected with the centrality of Jesus. That is why this return to the Bible is so foundational for the renewal of the Church. So *Dei verbum* says that Christ 'is himself both the mediator and the sum total of Revelation' (para. 2).

This correlation between the Bible and the person of Jesus is demonstrated most clearly in the term 'Word of God'. In the Scriptures, the eternal Son of God, who takes on human flesh, is called the Word of God. 'In the beginning was the Word, and the Word was with God, and the Word was God' (John 1:1). Then, some verses later, 'And the Word became flesh and dwelt among us, full of grace and truth; we have beheld his glory, glory as of the only Son from the Father' (John 1:14).[4]   And in one of the visions of the Lord in the book of Revelation, we are told, 'He is clad in a robe dipped in blood, and the name by which he is called is The Word of God' (Rev. 19:13).

So the Catechism has a heading 'Christ - the Unique Word of Sacred Scripture'.[5] This idea that God has one Word, and that word is Jesus, is based on the beginning of the letter to the Hebrews: 'In many and various ways God spoke of old to our fathers by the prophets; but in these last days he has spoken to us by a Son, whom he appointed the heir of all things, through whom also he created the world' (Heb. 1:1-2). So the Catechism states: 'Through all the words of Sacred Scripture, God speaks only one single Word, his one Utterance in whom he expresses himself completely' (para. 102). This is the same truth that Paul expresses in different language, when he says that in Christ 'are hid all the treasures of wisdom and knowledge' (Col. 2:3) and in him 'the whole fullness of deity dwells bodily' (Col. 2:9).

In the Scriptures, the written Word, we meet Jesus Christ, the Word in person. From the Scriptures, through the Holy Spirit, we know Jesus Christ. The bishops at Vatican II urged 'all the Christian faithful...to learn "the surpassing knowledge of Jesus Christ" (Phil. 3:8) by frequent reading of the divine Scriptures' (DV, para. 24). And they go on to quote the famous saying of St Jerome, 'Ignorance of the Scriptures is ignorance of Christ.'

In the Scriptures, the four Gospels have a special place 'because they are our principal source for the life and teaching of the Incarnate Word, our Saviour' (DV, para. 18).

Often students of theology may be more attracted to the teaching epistles, because they are more directly doctrinal. But when we recognize that the knowledge of Our Lord is the 'one thing necessary', then we will give a pride of place to the Gospels. In one way, we can say that the more difficult passages in the Gospels are to understand, the more important it is that we meditate on them, for they reflect most clearly how the thoughts of Jesus are higher than our thoughts - just as the Lord said to the prophet Isaiah: 'For as the heavens are higher than the earth, so are my ways higher than your ways and my thoughts than your thoughts' (Is. 55: 9). It is to honour the special place of the Gospels that in the liturgy there is always a reading from one of the Gospels, and that the whole congregation stands for that reading.

Access to All the Faithful

The Council recommended all Catholics to read the Bible, because the Word of God is our food, and we need to eat this food regularly. We can see in this recommendation an overcoming of the fear so widespread in the Catholic leadership after the Reformation that it was dangerous to allow Catholics unrestricted access to the Bible. Catholics of an older generation will certainly have heard comments like, 'You can defend any kind of doctrine from the Bible'; 'Protestants believe in the right of private interpretation, which means each person becomes his own Pope'; 'the Bible is too complicated for ordinary people to understand'. These remarks reflect a mentality that is no longer acceptable.

The Catholic who truly feeds on the Bible as the Word of God does so in the context of a liturgy-centred life. Far from individual Bible readers being left without any framework for understanding this complex work, the Church's liturgy provides the right Christian framework of understanding. The Trinitarian structure of the liturgy, its centredness on the paschal mystery of Jesus' death and resurrection, the relationship between the Old and the New Testaments, all these aspects of the liturgy shape our Catholic reading of the Bible.

However, this liturgical context underlines the importance of the homily that opens up the Scriptures to the people. In a renewed Church, an increasing number of the Catholics who come to week-day Mass also read the Scriptures daily. These people are thirsty both for the body of the Lord and for his Word. These feed each other.

The Need for a Biblical Theology

The bishops made clear the importance of the Scriptures for all Catholic theology. 'Sacred theology relies on the written Word of God, taken together with sacred Tradition, as on a permanent foundation. By this Word it is most firmly strengthened and constantly rejuvenated, as it searches out, under the light of faith, the full truth stored up in the mystery of Christ. Therefore, the "study of the sacred page" should be the very soul of sacred theology' (DV, para. 24).

The Catholic theology of the Counter-Reformation could not be said to have been soaked in the Scriptures. Rather, the use of the Bible was largely polemical, seeking in the sacred text arguments to use against the Protestants. The starting point for understanding was rarely the biblical text. Such a theology does not nourish the soul or the spiritual life. In fact, the original meaning of theology is 'the science of God', that is, the knowledge of God that comes from union with Christ and the working of the Holy Spirit. For the Fathers of the Church, theology was a practical and spiritual science, issuing from contemplative prayer, so that in the East the deepest of the evangelists, St John, was called 'St John the Theologian'.[6] Renewal of the Church requires a new integration of the Christian's life of the Spirit in the Church and a theological reflection issuing from that life and deepening it.

The Council's decrees on the Renewal of Religious Life and the Life of Priests state that the primary source for their formation and knowledge is the reading and meditation of the Scriptures.[7] The decree on the Training of Priests insists that 'Spiritual formation should be closely associated with doctrinal and pastoral formation…in such a way that the students may learn to live in intimate and unceasing union with God the Father through his Son Jesus Christ, in the Holy Spirit' (*Optatam totius*, para. 8). 'Students should receive a most careful training in holy Scripture, which should be the soul...of all theology' (OT, para. 16). In the study of dogmatic theology 'biblical themes should have first place' (OT, para. 16). In fact, making the Scriptures central in life and studies is a huge task, because it takes time to change the patterns of centuries. It should not surprise us that this is a task that still remains largely unfulfilled.

Renewal of the Church then requires a new attention to the Scriptures as the Word of God. It requires first lives that are fed by the Word and centred on Jesus Christ. But this then requires a renewed theology, both to protect and to further stimulate the new life of the Spirit. We can even say that whatever in the Church is not directly fed by the Scriptures will not be enlivened by the Holy Spirit.

Notes

[1] See, in particular, Chapters Nine, Twelve and Thirteen.

[2] Thus, the liturgies for the feasts of the Immaculate Conception and the Assumption of Our Lady contain many biblical passages that throw light on and point to these realities.

[3] 'She [the Church] never ceases to present to the faithful the bread of life, taken from the one table of God's Word and Christ's Body' (CCC, para. 103).

[4] See also the reference to the 'word of life' in 1 John 1:1.

[5] First heading in Part I, Article 3 on 'Sacred Scripture'.

[6] See CCC, para. 236.

[7] *Perfectae caritatis*, para. 6; *Presbyterorum ordinis*, para. 19.

Church *Forward*

CHAPTER FOUR
The Dignity of the Human Person

Recognition of the dignity of each human person is foundational for authentic renewal in the Church. Faith is essentially a free act. The Church has to be a model of human freedom if it is to be a convincing sign of the Kingdom of God.

There can be no real renewal of the Church without honouring the dignity of the human person. Here is another area where there has been a huge change in the Catholic Church, the scope of which has been masked by our emphasis on continuity and an uncritical reading of past history. In fact, the commitment of the Catholic Church to the defence of human rights for all peoples is a modern phenomenon that would have astonished such nineteenth-century Popes as Gregory XVI and Pius IX. The extent of this change is a measure of the depth of the renewal that the Holy Spirit is working in the Church.

The Catholic Church of the Counter-Reformation and of the 'Counter-Revolution' was a Church defending her own authority and the rights of the church institution. The first official moves away from this preoccupation came with Pope Leo XIII and the beginnings of Catholic Social Teaching. With Leo XIII's teaching in *Rerum novarum* (1891) on the rights of workers, including the right to a just wage and the right to form trade unions, the Church began to move away from an instinctive siding with traditional authority and to express a concern for the oppressed and the suffering.

A real concern for the world and its peoples, and not just for the Catholic population, was present in the efforts of Benedict XV and Pius XII to end war and to restore peace. But the old instincts to focus on the rights of Catholics alone did not die easily, as can be seen from the rather shocking protests of some Catholic authorities against the Nazi arrests of Jews baptized as Catholics, when they were not raising their voice against the oppression and extermination of the Jews as a whole.

As already noted, the pontificate of Blessed John XXIII heralded a new approach of the Catholic Church towards the dignity of the human person. Both in his life-style and his way of treating all people, as well as in his teaching on human rights, Pope John upheld the dignity of every human being. But it was with the Second Vatican Council that a coherent official teaching emerged concerning the role of the human person which would have application in society as a whole (the dignity of every human person) and in the Church (the dignity of all the baptized).

This transformation in Catholic teaching necessitated two major and related developments. The first was a change in philosophy: the change from a focus on things in themselves to a focus on the unique dignity of the human person. The second was a change in ecclesiology: the change from an authoritarian Church to a servant Church - still with authority, but not authority as understood in the world. The first will be treated in this chapter, the second in the next.

From Things to the Person

In the teaching of Vatican II, there was a shift from truth expressed in nature to truth embodied in the human person. The inherited method focused on nature and the 'essence' of things. Moral right and moral wrong were determined by accordance with or opposition to 'nature'. This approach did not do justice to the uniqueness of the human person, which is characterized by the capacity to love and to form relationships within society. So, with the Council, there is a new awareness of the dignity of every human being, and that human salvation depends on relationships, first with God and then with each other.

This opening up of the Church to the wonder of the human person required a turning away from preoccupation with the church institution. Almost all the draft documents prepared for the Council had been concerned with the inner life of the Church. But the church leaders closest in spirit to John XXIII understood the Council as a unique opportunity for the Church to speak a word of hope to the contemporary world. Towards the end of the first session, Cardinal Léon-Joseph Suenens of Malines, the primate of Belgium, proposed that the Council deal first with the Church *ad intra* (in herself) and then with the Church *ad extra* (in relation to the world). The credibility of the Church depends on speaking to the needs, the hopes and the suffering of the contemporary world. From this proposal was to emerge the Pastoral Constitution on the Church in the Modern World, known as *Gaudium et spes*.[1] The new spirit was to be expressed in its opening words: 'The joy and hope, the grief and anguish of the men of our time, especially of those who are poor or afflicted in any way, are the joy and hope, the grief and anguish of the followers of Christ as well' (para. 1).

However, John XXIII died before progress was made on this proposal. Cardinal Montini, who had strongly supported the Suenens proposal, was elected Pope in June 1963 and took the name of Paul VI. Even before *Gaudium et spes* was published (1965), Pope Paul VI would take up and nail in place another fundamental element for renewal with a new focus on the human person. This was the way of dialogue, proposed in his first encyclical letter, *Ecclesiam suam* (1964).

In *Ecclesiam suam*, Paul VI presented his vision for the renewal of the Catholic Church. The three tasks for the Church are: Self-Awareness, Renewal and Dialogue. A greater self-awareness of the Church, both of her riches and of her needs, leads to renewal. Renewal requires and leads to dialogue.

The Pope grounds dialogue in the character of God and of the Lord Jesus. 'God Himself took the initiative in the dialogue of salvation. "He has first loved us" (1 John 4:10). We, therefore, must be the first to ask for a dialogue with men, without waiting to be summoned to it by others' (ES, para. 72). So, for Paul VI, dialogue has to be the way of the Catholic Church. He would have been well aware that dialogue had not been prominent in the past comportment of the Catholic Church. Maybe this is why he makes a specific point of dialogue being 'catholic'. 'The dialogue of salvation was made accessible to all. It applied to everyone without distinction. Hence our dialogue too should be as universal as we can make it. That is to say, it must be catholic' (ES, para. 76).

Thus, Paul VI does not just dialogue with those people who are closest to the Catholic Church 'The dialogue of salvation did not depend on the merits of those with whom it was initiated, nor on the results it would be likely to achieve. "Those who are well have no need of a physician" (Luke 5: 31). Neither, therefore, should we set limits to our dialogue or seek in it our own advantage' (ES, para. 74). Dialogue is the way for the Catholic Church, because it is the only way to treat all human persons with dignity. To treat everyone with dignity is to follow the example of Jesus. It is to enter into dialogue with the intentions and the motivation of Jesus himself. 'The dialogue of salvation sprang from the goodness and the love of God. "God so loved the world that he gave his only Son" (John 3:16). Our inducement, therefore, to enter into this dialogue must be nothing other than a love which is ardent and sincere' (ES, para. 73).

This vision of dialogue was then taken up in the Council's Constitution on the Church in the Modern World (*Gaudium et spes*), that deals first with 'The Dignity of the Human Person' (Part I, Chapter 1). Besides pointing to the dignity of human intelligence, truth and wisdom (para. 15), this chapter speaks of the dignity of moral conscience: 'For man has in his heart a law inscribed by God. His dignity lies in observing this law, and by it he will be judged. His conscience is man's most secret core, and his sanctuary. There he is alone with God whose voice echoes in his depths. By conscience, in a wonderful way, that law is made known which is fulfilled in the love of God and of one's neighbour' (para. 16). This paragraph steers a careful path between an exaltation of conscience as an autonomous activity and a reduction of conscience to the duty of obeying external authority.

In consequence of this acceptance of dialogue, the Catholic Church since Vatican II has structured its relationships with all those outside the Catholic communion on the basis of dialogue. So there are in the Vatican Pontifical Councils for the Promotion of the Unity of Christians (dialogue with other Christian Churches and ecclesial communities); for Inter-religious Dialogue (dialogue with non-Christian religions); and for Culture (a development from the dialogue with unbelievers).[2]

Religious Liberty

Another sea-change in Catholic attitudes came with *Dignitatis humanae*, the Council's Declaration on Religious Liberty. In fact, religious liberty had been one of the ideas denounced by Popes of the nineteenth century in their defence of the old social order. 'This opposition arose because freedom of conscience was being urged as a freedom from "divine law".' But it is an absolutely necessary element in the Church's turn to the dignity of the human person.

The Declaration on Religious Liberty has two main thrusts, both essential for the proper flourishing of the human person. The first is the right to exercise one's religious faith in society, and to be free from state control and coercion. Here, the voice of bishops suffering under Communist oppression was heard. The Catholic authorities had often protested in the past against secular interference in church affairs, but earlier protests had been conflicts of authority: Pope versus Emperor and Church versus State. Now there is a different focus: a deeper understanding of Church and society is formulated with its foundation in the dignity and the uniqueness of the human person.

The second thrust of *Dignitatis humanae* is the insistence that 'the act of faith is of its very nature a free act' (para. 10). Therefore, 'nobody is to be forced to embrace the faith against his will' (para. 10). This recognition has many implications: all kinds of pressure to 'convert' are to be avoided. We can think here of the huge pressure to convert often placed in the past on others wanting to marry a Catholic, a pressure coming not only from restrictive legislation on mixed marriages, but often more strongly from the family of the Catholic party. In earlier epochs, there was the pressure to 'convert' to the faith of the prince, wherever the adage *eius regio cuius religio*[3] held sway. There were also numerous occasions when the Jewish people were offered the choice of 'conversion' or expulsion, as in Spain in 1492. The Catholic Church is now saying that we cannot allow such things to happen again.

This document led to immediate changes in the treatment of Protestant Christians in some predominantly Catholic nations, such as Spain, Portugal and Colombia. Prior to the Council, theologians had argued that 'error has no rights'. Therefore, Protestant churches had no rights: to hold services, to own property, to marry their people, etc. This had resulted in a double standard: in Protestant countries, the Catholic Church claimed her rights, and kept quiet about error having no rights; but in Catholic countries, the Protestants were treated as heretics, who had no rights. The dignity of the human person means that every human being has rights. It is not truth that has rights, but the human person and human societies.

The Presupposition for Renewal

Respecting the dignity of the human person is a key component in renewal. For renewal is the work of the Holy Spirit within each believer and within the church community. To respect the workings of the Holy Spirit requires an underlying respect for the conscience of each person. Christian renewal is renewal of faith. Faith requires freedom: freedom to act in faith, freedom to speak up and to express one's faith, and freedom to meet together and to organize the community of faith.

Pope John XXIII had such an impact on the world and provided such an impetus for the renewal of the Church because he had a profound respect for people, because he loved people as Jesus loved them - not only being willing to deal with them if their doctrine was sound or their morals were in good order. In this way, we can say that the respect for the dignity of every human person is grounded in the life of Jesus, who was himself the perfect reflection of the Father in heaven: 'But I say to you, Love your enemies and pray for those who persecute you, so that you may be sons of your Father who is in heaven; for he makes his sun rise on the evil and on the good, and sends rain on the just and on the unjust' (Matt. 5:44-45).

Notes

[1] Following the proposal of Cardinal Suenens, strongly endorsed by Cardinal Montini of Milan, a mixed commission was formed from the Theology and the Laity commissions to work on this document. One of the members of this commission was Mgr Wojtyla from Cracow, Poland, later to become Pope John Paul II.

[2] Benedict XVI may be thinking of merging the two last-named Councils as he has placed them under the same Cardinal President. The dialogue with Judaism does not come under the Pontifical Council for Inter-Religious Dialogue, but is the responsibility of a special commission linked to the office of the Council for Promoting Christian Unity.

[3] Roughly translated this means: whatever the region (of the prince), that is the religion (for the people).

CHAPTER FIVE
The Dignity of the Laity

The dignity of lay people in the Church is one with the dignity of the human person in society. The dignity of every Christian is rooted in their relationships with the Father, the Son and the Holy Spirit, that are established and symbolized in the sacrament of baptism. The dignity of the laity involves the call of each Christian to holiness of life and is enhanced by the charisms conferred on all for the good of the whole Church.

Although the Council's teaching on the dignity of the human person came in the final session, a year after the promulgation of the Constitution on the Church, there is a total congruity between this teaching and what *Lumen gentium* teaches concerning the laity. It would be illogical to affirm the dignity of every human person and the rights that go with that dignity, and not to affirm the dignity of lay people within the Church. The new respect for the laity expressed by the Council has its philosophical grounds in the dignity of each human person, but it also has a theological foundation in a new appreciation for the sacrament of baptism, and the presence and work of the Holy Spirit in every Christian. So a renewal of the Church is impossible without a recognition of the dignity of lay people and an acceptance of their proper role within the Church.

John Henry Newman was a prophetic voice of the nineteenth century, anticipating a century in advance the direction of Vatican II. His appreciation for the laity is an important instance. In 1859, Newman wrote a short essay entitled 'On Consulting the Faithful in Matters of Doctrine', which elicited disapproval in most clerical circles of the day, including Rome. He was developing the doctrine of the *sensus fidelium*, the instinct of the faithful for the truth of divine revelation, produced within them by the working of the Holy Spirit. Newman rejected a totally clerical view of the Church, which would see the duties of the laity totally in terms of obedience to the clergy. He wrote: 'Though the laity be but the reflection or echo of the clergy in matters of faith, yet there is something in the "pastorum et fidelium conspiratio" [the "conspiracy" of pastors and faithful], which is not in the pastors alone.'[1]

One strong opponent of Newman was Mgr Talbot, an English prelate in Rome, who professed an extreme clericalist (and aristocratic) mentality in a letter to Archbishop Manning of Westminster: 'What is the province of the laity? To hunt, to shoot, to entertain. These matters they understand, but to meddle with ecclesiastical matters they have no right at all.' But Newman saw clearly the dangers of a passive laity, ending his essay with a prophetic warning that when the teaching Church cuts off the laity from the study of doctrine and from her contemplation of the Lord, and simply requires an implicit faith in Catholic teaching, this will end up 'in the educated classes...in indifference, and in the poorer in superstition'.[2]

The laity began to receive more attention in the time of Pius XI (1922-39). This was the period when new lay movements like the Young Christian Workers and the Legion of Mary were formed. This new interest on the part of Pope and bishops represented in part a reaction to the Communist Revolution in Russia. The thinking was, 'If we don't do something to activate the masses, the Communists will get there first.' But it also reflected the political trends in which there was a move away from rule by monarchy and aristocracy towards popular democracy in which every adult citizen has the vote. The advance of democracy had made the church authorities very cautious in opening up to lay activism, as it was constantly made clear that the Church is not a democracy; its structure is essentially hierarchical.

The 'lay apostolate' was well established by the time of Vatican II. In fact, one of Pius XII's last major addresses was to a world congress of the lay apostolate. But the Council would not just endorse the lay apostolate, it would transform the understanding of the place of the laity in the Church. The lay apostolate before the Council had largely been a recruitment of zealous laity to help the clergy in their ministry. This was most obvious in Catholic Action, with its tight ties to the hierarchy, and clear too in the spirituality of the Legion of Mary. The transformation at Vatican II was to root the calling of the laity in baptism, and to insist that while Catholic lay people need to respect the authority of Pope, bishop and priest, their essential activity as baptized believers does not depend on being commissioned or given permission by a priest or bishop.

The Constitution on the Church says that the laity 'in their own way share in the priestly, prophetic and kingly office of Christ' (LG, para. 31). Every Christian receives the gift of the Holy Spirit and is conformed to Jesus Christ as a son or daughter of the Father. When we understand what this means, we cannot regard being a lay Christian as an inferior calling. When the Council deals with the laity's prophetic role, it speaks of their role as witnesses and as 'heralds of the faith'. This is the one place in *Lumen gentium* that speaks of 'evangelization'.[3] The laity do not need permission to pray, to witness to their faith, or to meet with other Christians. So, this Council teaching on the laity would lead some twenty years later to a formulation for the first time in Catholic history of the right of all the baptized to meet and to form associations.[4]

The gift of the Holy Spirit to each Christian knocks on the head the widespread Catholic assumption that if one wants to be holy, one should become a priest, a monk or a nun. All the baptized are called to holiness of life. So *Lumen gentium* has a chapter on 'The Call to Holiness' between the chapter on 'The Laity' and that on 'Religious'. All lay people are called to holiness, and this is rooted in their baptism. The particular call of religious has to be understood within this general call to holiness, and not as the only real call to be holy. Paradoxically, the way for this universal call to holiness had been prepared by a religious, St Thérèse of Lisieux, in her teaching on the 'Little Way', the way of love, that is open to all.

At Vatican II, charisms enter into the Catholic understanding of the Church. This has major importance for the laity. Charism was another term unfamiliar to Catholics before the Council. It is in fact a biblical term meaning gifts and endowments freely given by God to any Christian for the good of the Church. Now the bishops recognize that God bestows such charisms, that are given to all kinds of believers and are presented as an essential part of the equipment of the Church. The Holy Spirit 'distributes special graces among the faithful of every rank' (LG, para. 12). This is another decisive step away from a clericalist view of the Church and her ministry. 'By these gifts he makes them [the faithful] fit and ready to undertake various tasks and offices for the renewal and building up of the Church, as it is written, "the manifestation of the Spirit is given to everyone for profit" (1 Cor. 12:7)' (para. 12). From the gift of these charisms, 'there arises for each of the faithful the right and the duty of exercising them in the Church and in the world for the good of men and the development of the Church, of exercising them in the freedom of the Holy Spirit who "breathes where he wills" (Jn 3:8)'.[5] This language of rights and duties of lay people to exercise their charisms and the emphasis on the freedom of the Spirit, both in the conferring of charisms and in their exercise, is still unfamiliar to most Catholics, even within the Catholic charismatic renewal, where charisms are recognized and expected.

With this teaching on the charisms, we find a deeper theological element in the active contribution of the laity to the life and mission of the church. The universal call to holiness can be misunderstood as a passive role for the laity: just loving others and praying instead of hunting, shooting and fishing! The notion of charisms given to all underlines the positive contribution of all church members to her mission. This again shifts the responsibility of the ordained ministry from control to discernment. So the responsibility of the pastors here is to 'recognize the contribution [of the laity] and charisms' (LG, para. 31).

A Tension

During the pre-Vatican II encouragement of the lay apostolate, it was taught that the role of the laity is found in the secular world, in contrast to the role of clergy and religious which is exercised in the Church. This understanding was taken up and expressed in *Lumen gentium*: 'But by reason of their special vocation it belongs to the laity to seek the kingdom of God by engaging in temporal affairs and directing them according to God's will' (para. 31). This is further developed in the Decree on the Apostolate of Lay People: 'Laymen ought to take on themselves as their distinctive task this renewal of the temporal order' (AA, para. 7). In many ways, this understanding of the role of the laity underpins *Gaudium et spes* in its more detailed treatment of the relationship of the Church to the world, and its addressing specific areas of human activity in the world and in society.[6]

But in the Vatican II documents one can also find the beginnings of a less 'secular' view of the laity. This is most obvious in the passages on charisms granted in principle to believers from all walks in the Church, for example in the passage from *Lumen gentium* cited above: 'By these gifts he makes them [the faithful] fit and ready to undertake various tasks and offices for the renewal and building up of the Church'. In the years after the Council, we see this tension increase with the growth of the new ecclesial movements,[7] with the rise of explicit Catholic evangelization[8] and with the growing involvement of lay people in all aspects of the Church's mission, except those restricted to ordained ministers.

This tension shows that the earlier Catholic assignment of the secular world as the proper sphere of the laity often masked a form of clericalism that was in effect excluding the laity from much meaningful participation in the mission of the Church. It seems to have been based on the widespread assumption that the lay witness to the person of Christ is indirect and not explicit, e.g. by bearing witness to Christian principles and values. Such a view that the Church is divided up into ordained clergy, who speak openly of Christ and religion (in church), and laity, whose witness to Christ in the world is indirect, is no longer tenable and is clearly incompatible with the teachings of Vatican II. Obviously, it remains true that dedicated laity have an important and unique role to play in society, particularly by witnessing to Christian principles and values, and that this encouragement from the Church can be positive and honouring. But the renewing work of the Holy Spirit in the Church inevitably challenges all forms of clericalism. The tension between lay involvement in society and lay involvement in the activities of the Church is a necessary one in order to protect the Church not only from clericalism, but also from distancing itself from the world.

Notes

[1] John Henry Newman, *On Consulting the Faithful in Matters of Doctrine*, ed. John Coulson (London, 1961: Geoffrey Chapman), p. 106.

[2] Ibid., p. 106.

[3] See also Chapter Nine.

[4] See *The Code of Canon Law,* paras. 215-216.

[5] See also AA, para. 3.

[6] The areas treated in Part II of *Gaudium et spes* are: Marriage and Family Life; Culture; Economic and Social Life; the Political Community; Fostering of Peace and Establishment of a Community of Nations.

[7] See Chapter Twelve.

[8] See Chapter Nine.

Church *Forward*

CHAPTER SIX
Christian Unity

Renewal of the Church is inseparable from ecumenism, and ecumenism is inseparable from renewal. Both require a new focus on Jesus as the centre of all Christian faith. Both church communities and all Christians need this constant conversion to Christ. This is only possible through the Holy Spirit.

When John XXIII announced the summoning of an 'Ecumenical Council', many Christians thought that Christian unity was the sole or central purpose of the Council. In fact, 'Ecumenical Council' had long been a technical Catholic term for a General Council bringing together all the bishops of the Catholic Church. Modern usage referring to the movement for Christian unity only dates from the start of the twentieth century. But in fact, the cause of unity did have a place from the beginning in Pope John's plans for the Council.

John XXIII had had a heart for Christian unity since his years as apostolic delegate in Bulgaria and in Istanbul, when he was first in a largely Orthodox nation and subsequently at the centre of the Orthodox world. He became aware of the great treasures and riches present in the Orthodox tradition. His deep sense that the cause of unity and the renewal of the Catholic Church were ultimately inseparable dates from these years.

The concern for Christian unity was totally in the logic of the Council. It is in the logic of respect for the dignity of each human person, for we can no longer treat Christians who belong to other Churches as 'heretics' and 'non-persons'. It is in the logic of recognizing the call to holiness in all the baptized, for the members of other Christian Churches are also baptized. They also are sons and daughters of the same Father in the one Christ. It is in the logic of giving the Word of God its rightful place, for other Christians have often shown a greater love for the Sacred Scriptures than we Catholics have done. How can we honour the Scriptures and not honour those who have loved these same Scriptures?

From Fear to Trust

When people go through some traumatic experience, they are often left with a great fear. They are afraid of a repetition of their pain and loss. Any episode or person reminding them of their trauma can set off the fear within them. It was the same with the Catholic Church after the Reformation. The Protestant Reformation was a tremendous trauma for the Catholic Church. Whole nations and peoples were in revolt. There was a real danger that only a western Mediterranean fringe would remain Catholic. Yes, there had to be reform to remove the obvious abuses that had provoked the rebellion, and this was achieved, but the Church was left with major fears, including a fear of an open Bible and a fear of the Holy Spirit.

There was a Catholic fear of an open Bible because the Protestants appealed to the Bible against the authority and the teachings of the Catholic Church. While Protestants appealed to Scripture, Catholics appealed to tradition. So there grew up the idea among Catholics that reading the Bible is dangerous for lay people. In a parallel way, there was a fear of the Holy Spirit, as some Protestants had appealed to the Holy Spirit in support of their convictions. Here again, the defensive stand of the Catholic Church resulted in a conflict between those appealing to the Holy Spirit and those appealing to church authority. The former was subjective, the latter objective. In Spain the word *illuminados*, the illuminated ones, was synonymous with heresy. So good Catholics listened to the priest and the Pope, while seeking the light of the Holy Spirit was denounced as 'illuminism'.

The calling of the Council was itself a great act of trust in the Holy Spirit. John XXIII composed a prayer to the Holy Spirit for all Catholics to say in preparation for the Council.

He trusted the Holy Spirit to guide the bishops. Pope John understood the difference between trust and control. He rejected any temptation to try and control the Council. Similarly, the decision to open up the Bible to all the faithful and to recommend reading of the Scriptures was a decisive repudiation of the earlier fear. Casting off these fears has opened the doors to profound renewal in the Catholic Church.

The move from fear to trust required a new approach to the other Christian Churches. It meant a change from rejection to dialogue. It meant listening to the convictions of the Orthodox and of the Protestants. It meant addressing the deepest complaints of the Protestant Reformers – not necessarily to agree with all of them, but to take their protest seriously. This was made possible by the invitation to the Council of observers from other Christian Churches and communities. The observers were able to attend the debates, they were given copies of the confidential documents, and they were able to discuss them with the bishops. While the observers were not allowed to address the Council themselves, their thoughts and convictions often found their way into the speeches of sympathetic bishops.

Conversion to a Christ-centredness

One of the major pioneers in ecumenical work had been a priest from Lyon, France – the Abbé Paul Couturier

(1881–1953). Couturier had been won to the cause of Christian unity through his pastoral work in Lyon for refugees from the Russian Revolution. He was impressed by their Orthodox faith and devotion. He became deeply convinced of the importance of prayer for Christian unity. But at that time - in the 1930s - it was forbidden for Catholics to pray with non-Catholics of any persuasion. The newly approved Chair of Unity Octave prayed explicitly for the return of dissident Christians to the see of Peter, a format that hardly any Protestant or Orthodox could ever accept. Couturier knew in his spirit that it had to be possible for all Christians to pray in the same way for Christian unity, so he sought light from the Lord on this dilemma.

Couturier received his answer from the high priestly prayer of Jesus in John, chapter 17. Here Jesus prayed that 'they may all be one, even as you, Father, are in me, and I in you, so that the world may believe that you have sent me.' Couturier saw that every Christian, of no matter what church affiliation, can pray for the unity for which Jesus prayed. So Couturier's formula was for all Christians to pray for the unity that Christ wills in the manner that he wills.

In retrospect, we can see that the Holy Spirit had shown the Abbé Couturier a key principle for the renewal of the Church. He transformed a Church-centred approach into a Christ-centred approach. But this transformation was not against the Church: it was not switching from a focus on the Church to an ignoring of the Church. Couturier was never an individualist. He always had a strong awareness of Christian faith as essentially ecclesial. The transformation was from a Church-centredness to an ecclesial Christ-centredness, that is to say, from a Church focusing on itself to a Church focusing on Christ.

This common prayer for Christian unity, following the model of John 17, was at the centre of what Couturier called 'spiritual ecumenism'. Although not immediately appreciated by all Catholics at the time, Couturier's 'spiritual ecumenism' was to be adopted thirty years later by the Catholic bishops at the Second Vatican Council. Paragraphs 6 to 8 of the Decree on Ecumenism (*Unitatis redintegratio*) represent a distillation of the core of Couturier's teaching on spiritual ecumenism. These principles of spiritual ecumenism can be summarized as follows:

- 'Every renewal of the Church essentially consists in an increase of fidelity to her own calling' (UR, para. 6).
- The Church [on earth] is summoned to a continual reformation. [Here there is a Catholic acceptance of the Reformation principle that the Church is always in need of reformation, *Ecclesia semper reformanda*.] (UR, para. 6).
- Ecumenism requires interior conversion (UR, para. 7).
- 'This change of heart and holiness of life, along with public and private prayer for the unity of Christians, should be regarded as the soul of the whole ecumenical

movement, and merits the name "spiritual ecumenism"' (UR, para. 8).

In other words, it is as each Church and confession becomes more faithful to Jesus Christ, and the lives of its members are more conformed to the life of Christ, that they will be drawn into the unity for which Jesus prayed. Here was no compromise, as the first critics of Couturier feared, but a profound call to renewal. Renewal of the Church is inseparable from ecumenism, and ecumenism is inseparable from renewal.

Corporate Reconciliation not Individual Submission

The decree on Ecumenism opened a major door for reconciliation when it recognized that the Holy Spirit is at work in other Christian Churches and communities. Before the Council, the widespread assumption among Catholics had been - especially in English-speaking countries where Catholics were a minority - that corporate reunion with Protestant Churches was an illusion and that the only way forward was for Protestant Christians to submit to Rome individually and be 'converted'.

The bishops stated: 'some, even very many, of the most significant elements and endowments which together go to build up and give life to the Church itself, can exist outside the visible boundaries of the Catholic Church: the written Word of God; the life of grace; faith, hope and charity, with the other interior gifts of the Holy Spirit, as well as visible elements' (UR, para. 3). This is being said not just of individual Christians outside the Catholic Church, but of their communities of faith. Thus, despite various deficiencies, these churchly (ecclesial) communities 'have been by no means deprived of significance in the mystery of salvation' and the Holy Spirit 'has not refrained from using them as means of salvation' (UR, para. 3).

This evaluation of other Christian church communities is really a liberation from what in retrospect can be seen as an ideological narrowness. As Catholics, we are now free to approach other Christians and their communities and to appreciate and evaluate them as they are - in their gracedness and in their weakness. We can learn not to interpret them totally through our own categories. The role that Protestant denominations and their ministries play in the salvation of their members is a matter for objective study, not for a priori denial. This openness to grace is an important ingredient in renewal, because it frees us to learn from other Christians and to be blessed by their gifts. This in turn frees them to learn from us and to be blessed by our gifts.

Baptism as Bond of Unity

The third chapter of the Decree on Ecumenism is divided into two parts: the first on the Churches of the East, and the second on those stemming from the Protestant Reformation. The first group are recognized as Churches within the apostolic succession of ministry and sacraments. The Council recognized in solemn language that the Churches of the East 'have the power to govern themselves according to their own disciplines' (UR, para. 16), and thus any reunion with the Catholic Church would not require direct government from Rome. Indeed, the bishops confess that 'this traditional principle...has not always been observed', a reference to the latinization of Eastern Catholic churches at some periods in the past. There is also an acknowledgment that in some areas the East, and in others the West, has come 'nearer to a full appreciation of some aspects of a mystery of revelation than the other' (UR, para. 17).

As far as relations with the Protestant world is concerned, the Council emphasizes the common bond of baptism, administered according to the Lord's intention (meaning in effect with the Trinitarian formula of Matthew 28:19). 'Baptism...constitutes the sacramental bond of unity existing among all who through it are reborn' (UR, para. 22). For the Protestant Churches and communities whose ministry is not recognized by the Catholic Church, the recognition of a sacramental foundation in a commonly-recognized baptism was important. But while this statement is acceptable to the historic Reformation Churches that practise infant baptism (such as the Anglicans, the Lutherans and the Reformed), it has some limitations which were not immediately recognized. In particular, it does not commend itself to those many Christians who do not believe in baptismal regeneration and who generally practise believers' baptism of adults (such as Baptists, Mennonites, Pentecostals and other newer groupings).[1]

Dialogue and Collaboration

The Council's practical recommendations for a new era in inter-church relations focused on two activities: dialogue and collaboration. Dialogue was envisaged as meetings of qualified and appointed theologians to 'better understand the outlook of our separated brethren and more aptly present our own belief' (UR, para. 9). While the Council insists that 'doctrine be presented in its entirety', it is also recognized - a significantly new statement - that 'in Catholic doctrine there exists an order or 'hierarchy' of truths, since they vary in their relation to the foundation of the Christian faith' (UR, para. 11). The hierarchy of truths will be a key notion for church renewal, because the recognition that there are both central doctrines and derivative doctrines opens the way to understanding that there can only be spiritual renewal when the central doctrines that form the foundation are given their rightful place.

Collaboration in good between all peoples is praiseworthy, but 'cooperation among Christians vividly expresses that bond, which already unites them, and it sets in clearer relief the features of Christ the Servant' (UR, para. 12). At this initial stage, the collaboration envisaged is restricted to 'social matters', but we need to remember that this decree was issued against a background where, in most parts of the world, there was no collaboration at all between the Catholic Church and other Christians. One of the first areas in which collaboration developed was in Bible translations, with new relations being established between the Catholic Federation for the Biblical Apostolate and various Protestant Bible Societies. In the English-speaking world it led to a Catholic edition of the Revised Standard Version.

The closing words of the Decree on Ecumenism, however, recognize the essentially dynamic character of the ecumenical movement, and the need not to obstruct 'the ways of divine Providence' and not to prejudge 'the future inspirations of the Holy Spirit'. 'This holy objective... transcends human powers and gifts' (UR, para. 24). The Council was the beginning of the ecumenical journey for the Catholic Church. It will not be surprising that it will feature prominently in new developments after the Council.[2]

Notes

[1] On this question, see Chapter Fourteen.
[2] See especially Chapters Eleven and Twelve.

CHAPTER SEVEN
The Jewish People

Renewal of the Church requires a return to the biblical roots. These roots are Jewish. When the Church encounters the Jewish people, she is faced in some way by her own origins. Renewal of the Church cannot bypass the issue of the Jewish people and their place in God's eternal plan.

How is it that, for the first time in history, a Council of the Church came to address theologically the question of the Jewish people and their place in God's plan? The short answer is Pope John XXIII. During his service as apostolic delegate in Bulgaria and in Istanbul, he had experienced at first hand the sufferings of the Jews under Nazi tyranny. When details of deportations and other atrocities were reported, Archbishop Roncalli never delegated these matters, but took action himself. He risked his reputation and position by providing thousands of Turkish visas, 'temporary' baptismal certificates and immigration documents to Jews seeking to flee the Nazi extermination machine. It is estimated that Archbishop Roncalli issued as many as 80,000 documents to needy Jews, thus helping to save many lives.

So it seems certain that it was in the heart of John XXIII that the Council should treat this question. But, as was characteristic of Pope John, he does not seem to have had any precise plans at the start of his papacy. The interest aroused by the calling of the Council extended beyond the Christian world. Jewish leaders sensed the possibility of a momentous change for the better, responding warmly to the Pope's decision to delete words offensive to the Jews from the Good Friday liturgy. As always, the Jewish people were highly sensitive to changes in Rome that could affect their lot. For them, Good Friday had often been a day of danger from Christian mobs, stirred up by sermons accusing the Jews of being 'God-killers'.

Probably decisive for the Pope was a visit paid to the Vatican in June 1960 by a leading Jewish historian from France, Jules Isaac. Monsieur Isaac presented John XXIII with a dossier concerned with the correction of anti-Jewish elements in Christian teaching. By this time, the Pope had received at least two requests from Catholic scholars along the same lines.[1] Only three months later in September 1960, the Pope commissioned Cardinal Bea in his capacity as President of the Secretariat for Promoting Christian Unity to prepare a theological document on the relationship between the Church and the people of Israel.

The decision to entrust this work to Cardinal Bea was both politically and theologically wise and reflected John XXIII's personal confidence in the German cardinal, both as a scholar and as a man of spiritual integrity. The role of Cardinal Bea meant that the Jewish question first appeared on the Council's agenda as part of the draft document on Ecumenism that was presented to the bishops in November 1963. However, powerful pressures, political and theological, caused the teaching on the Jewish people to be transferred to another document, the Declaration on Non-Christian Religions.[2]

The Council's Teaching

The teaching on the status of the Jewish people eventually constituted paragraph 4 of the Declaration on Non-Christian Religions, known as *Nostra aetate*. Of the five paragraphs of this short document, the fourth is much the longest and the most detailed. It represents a transformation in the attitude of the Catholic Church to the Jewish people. From this paragraph, four key points can be singled out as markers for this new Catholic approach:

1. The Catholic Church 'deplores all hatreds, persecutions, displays of anti-Semitism levelled at any time or from any source against the Jews.'

This point was the easiest for the bishops to agree. However, this statement has explosive content, as we shall see when we come to a later chapter on Catholic repentance for sins of the past.[3] The words 'at any time' and 'from any source' clearly mean that the anti-Semitic elements in Catholic history must also be deplored.

2. The Jewish people as a whole are not to be accused of 'deicide', as had often happened in the past. 'Neither all Jews indiscriminately at that time, nor Jews today, can be charged with the crimes committed during his [Jesus'] passion.'

In fact, the Roman Catechism of 1570, issued following the Council of Trent, had taught that 'sinners were the authors and the ministers of all the sufferings that the divine Redeemer endured.'[4] This passage was later cited in the *Catechism of the Catholic Church*, paragraph 598. The 1994 Catechism also provided a more detailed refutation of the 'deicide' accusation under the heading 'Jews are not collectively responsible for Jesus' death'.[5]

3. God has not rejected the Jewish people. 'It is true that the Church is the new people of God, yet the Jews should not be spoken of as rejected or accursed as if this followed from holy Scripture.' The covenant of the Lord with the people of Israel has not been revoked. 'Paul maintains that the Jews remain very dear to God, for the sake of the patriarchs, since God does not take back the gifts he bestowed or the choice he made.'[6]

With these historic words, the Catholic Church brings to an official end the age-long idea that God had rejected the Jewish people, because they had rejected Jesus. This wrong thinking, known as 'replacement teaching', 'substitution teaching' or 'supersessionism', i.e. that the Church had taken the place of the Jews, had often been expressed in inflammatory preaching that had stirred up Catholic peoples against the Jewish people.

In the years after the Council, this repudiation of replacement teaching has become more explicit. A Vatican document of 1985 states about the Jews: 'We must …rid ourselves of the traditional idea of a people punished, preserved as a living argument for Christian apologetic. It remains a chosen people, "the pure olive on which were grafted the branches of the wild olive which are the gentiles" (John Paul II, 6 March 1982, alluding to Rm 11:17-24).'[7] So, the revised liturgy for Good Friday speaks of the Jewish people simply as 'the people of the covenant'.

4. The roots of the Christian Church are to be found in the Jewish people: 'The Church of Christ acknowledges that in God's plan of salvation the beginning of her faith and election is to be found in the patriarchs, Moses and the prophets.' Therefore we cannot understand the Church properly if we do not recognize and honour these Jewish roots. Commenting later on the Council text, John Paul II stated: 'Thus it is understood that our two religious

communities are connected and closely related at the very level of their respective religious identities.'[8]

The Council declaration cites a passage from Paul's words about his kinsmen in the epistle to the Romans: 'they are Israelites, and to them belong the sonship, the glory, the covenants, the giving of the law, the worship, and the promises; to them belong the patriarchs, and of their race according to the flesh, is the Christ (Rom. 9:4-5).'[9] The clear meaning, notwithstanding the absence of the word 'belong' in the original Greek, is that these were still the privileges of the Jewish people.

This unique relationship between the Church and the Jewish people has been made more explicit since the Council. So, in 1986, on the first visit of a Bishop of Rome to a synagogue, John Paul II told the Jews of Rome: 'The Jewish religion is not "extrinsic" to us, but in a certain way is "intrinsic" to our own religion. With Judaism, therefore, we have a relationship which we do not have with any other religion. You are our dearly beloved brothers and, in a certain way, it could be said that you are our elder brothers.'[10]

A Huge Challenge

The Second Vatican Council was the first occasion in nearly two thousand years in which the Church had given an official teaching on the Jewish people. In fact, it is just as revolutionary as the teaching on access to the Scriptures and on the dignity of the human person. Just as both these new emphases are foundational for the renewal of the Church, so also is the Council's teaching on the Jewish people. This is no teaching on a marginal issue, peripheral to the major doctrinal issues concerning God, Christology, salvation, the Church and the sacraments.

The teaching on the Jewish people affects our understanding of the Scriptures. It affects our understanding of Jesus, Mary and the apostles. It affects our understanding of the Church. It affects our understanding of the eschatological completion. But because this is so new, it will take time, possibly several generations, for the Church to discover all the implications of *Nostra aetate*, paragraph 4. We can already see some of them in the more developed positions expressed in the *Catechism of the Catholic Church*.[11]

The Jews and Christian Unity

The origins of the Council's teaching on ecumenism and on the Jewish people indicate that there was an awareness of the inter-connectedness of these two topics. As mentioned, in the original plans the Decree on Ecumenism would have had five chapters, the eventual three in the final decree, plus a fourth on the Jews and a fifth on Religious Liberty. The explicit link between Christian unity and the Jewish people in the Council documents was thus lost, when the teaching on the Jews was moved to another document. But in the mind of Cardinal Bea, it was clear that there is a connection between Christian unity and Jewish-Christian relations. However, in the organizational structure of the Vatican, a connection remained since the Council for relations with the Jews has retained the connection with the Secretariat (now Pontifical Council) for Unity and does not come under the body responsible for relations with non-Christian religions. This connection expresses the truth that Jewish-Christian relations are 'intra-covenantal', within the mystery of divine election, and thus have a direct bearing on the unity of the People of God.

Unfortunately, *Unitatis redintegratio* in its final form makes no reference at all to the Jewish people, not even in its account of the origins of the Church. *Lumen gentium* has some references, but its sections on the birth of the Church are not as clear as the wording in *Nostra aetate* on the Jewish roots of the Church. This is a measure of the newness of the insights in *Nostra aetate*.

The importance of this question for church renewal will be most obvious when we return to the sources in Sacred Scripture and at the same time recognize the deeply Jewish character of the New Testament as well as of the Old. As all renewal is centred on the person of Jesus, the rediscovery of the Jewishness of Jesus is foundational for the renewal of the Church in all its aspects.

Notes

[1] From the Pontifical Biblical Institute in Rome, and the Institute of Judaco-Christian Studies at Seton Hall University in New Jersey, USA.

[2] This also happened to the Declaration on Religious Liberty.

[3] See Chapter Eleven.

[4] Roman Catechism, I, 5, 11.

[5] See para. 597.

[6] Cf. Rom. 11:28-29 (Council's citation).

[7] *Catholic Jewish Relations* (ed. Eugene Fisher and Klenicki), p. 47, para. 25. 'This people perseveres in spite of everything because they are the people of the Covenant, and despite human infidelities, the Lord is faithful to his Covenant' (Address of John Paul II to Symposium on 'The Roots of Anti-Judaism in the Christian Milieu', 31 October 1997 in Information Service - P.C.P.C.U. - Vatican City 1997/IV, p. 142).

[8] Response of Pope John Paul II to Representatives of Jewish Organizations, 12 March, 1979 (Fisher and Klenicki, p. 4).

[9] The word "belong", found twice in the translation, is missing in the original Greek.

[10] Fisher and Klenicki, p. 63. The year before, the Pope had spoken of 'a relation which could well be called a real "parentage" and which we have with that religious community alone' (p. 56).

[11] See, in particular, paras. 218-221, 528, 597-598, 674, 781, 839-840, 1096.

Church *Forward*

CHAPTER EIGHT
The Church as Communion

The Church is fellowship in Trinitarian communion. 'Our fellowship is with the Father and with his Son Jesus Christ'. (1 John 1:3). Renewal of the Church requires an ecclesiology of communion and an ever-deepening life of communion with and in the Holy Trinity, with fellow-Christians and with all other human beings.

The subject of the Church was never far from the centre of the Second Vatican Council. Pope John's vision was for the renewal of the Church. A Council for renewal required a renewed theology of the Church. The new attention to the Scriptures required a more biblically based theology of the Church. By starting with the worship of the Church, the Council made clear that the Church is most profoundly a people called to worship the living God. 'Through Christ, the Mediator, they [the faithful] should be drawn day by day in ever more perfect union with God and each other, so that finally God may be all in all' (SC, para. 48). The renewal of the liturgy focuses attention on the Church as communion. In this chapter, we will look in particular at how communion has emerged as a central concept in Catholic ecclesiology and how the reality of communion underpins the renewal of different aspects of church life: the collegiality of the bishops, laity, ecumenism, the understanding of the Jewish people, the role of Mary, the coming Kingdom.

From the Counter-Reformation reaction against the Protestant Reformation, Catholics learned to see the Church first as institution. This still persists in some of our terminology: for example, when we equate the Church with the hierarchy. However, institution should not be understood negatively. This institution passed on spiritual wisdom and riches from the past, it took care of our spiritual needs from the cradle to the grave, it protected us from much that is evil. But this emphasis had unfortunate side-effects: the Catholic faith easily became a religion of externals, a list of practices to perform and actions to avoid, and with the more pious a litany of devotional activities to accomplish. The Church was too easily seen as outside and above the people. The Christian life too easily became 'commodified', the grace of God too easily likened to 'things' that God gives, and the Church to a religious supermarket. The relationship of the devout to the Lord could become like that of a client to a supplier.

Of course, the lives of the saints who have glorified the Lord in every generation of the Church demonstrate that this objectivized religion was never the whole story. The saints and many others knew that their deepest honour was to be sons and daughters of the Father, incorporated into Christ his Son, and enlivened by the Holy Spirit. There were always scholars who understood that the Church is more than an institution founded by Jesus Christ. They were around especially in the milieux where the Fathers of the Church were known and loved, above all in the monasteries. This vision was still expressed, for example, in many of the readings used in the Roman Breviary, read by all priests and celebrated in religious houses every day. From time to time, theologians arose who presented this more biblical and patristic vision of the Church, often centred on the image of the Church as the Body of Christ. This trend had gathered momentum in the first half of the twentieth century, aided by the first steps in the renewal of Catholic biblical scholarship.[1] These developments received official backing in Pius XII's encyclical letter on the Church, *Mystici corporis christi* (1943). In this encyclical Pius XII moved Catholic ecclesiology away from a focus on the church institution to a more spiritual focus on the Church as the Body of Christ, while insisting on the basic identity of the spiritual body and the earthly institution. The Pope thus rejected any tendency to separate the spiritual and the institutional, as happens when people ignore or reject the institution and its authority by appealing to Christ and the Spirit. This position would be maintained by the Council, but his identification of the Body of Christ with the Roman Catholic Church would undergo significant modification.

A Trinitarian Vision

The Second Vatican Council's Constitution on the Church, *Lumen gentium*, was designed as the over-arching document of the Council into whose framework many of the Council's decrees would fit and from which their contents would flow.[2] But the cohesion of the conciliar documents is not primarily an organizational achievement but a coherence of theological vision. Only with such a vision could *Lumen gentium* form the basis for an authentic renewal of Catholic life.

This vision is first of all Trinitarian. The Council's teaching on the Church begins with the Trinity. There are consecutive paragraphs on the work of the Father, and of the Son and of the Holy Spirit. The theme running through this section is that the Church shares in the communion of the Trinity. Just as the Trinity is the most intense and unlimited inter-personal sharing, so in the Church the Holy Spirit brings Christians the most profound inter-personal love and communication - in Christ. This anchoring of the Church in the Trinitarian communion of God shows that the heart of Christian faith is relationship: first, our relationship with the Father, the Son and the Holy Spirit, and then our relationships with each other.

Here we find a major corrective to largely external religion. We cannot just understand our position as

Christians in terms of 'graces' that God gives. It is true that God gives graces or blessings, but above all God loves those who have become his sons and daughters in baptism. The Council's vision requires that all our faith-practice flow from our essential dignity as sons and daughters of the Father, baptized into Christ and indwelt by the Holy Spirit. This is at the heart of church renewal.

Secondly, the vision is itself ecclesial. The communion in the Church is not only a communion of individual Christians, but a communion of local churches. The local churches, the dioceses, themselves in their deepest reality a communion of life, are related to each other in bonds of communion. The institutional emphasis had easily led to the Catholic Church being understood simply as a worldwide institution. Fr Franciszek Blachnicki, the founder of the Oasis movement in Poland, has spoken of the theology of the Church moving from the concept of the *societas perfecta*, the 'perfect society', to that of the *communio sanctorum*, the 'communion of saints'.[3] The Council took us back to the New Testament, to remind us of the local church of a city, today a diocese,[4] and of the house or 'domestic' church. This rediscovery is closely connected with communion. The diocese is not just a branch of the universal Church. Rather, the universal Church is present in each local church. The Council taught that in 'the particular church', the diocese, 'the one, holy, catholic and apostolic Church of Christ is truly present' (*Christus dominus*, para. 11). It is in the local church that we live communion. Our relationship to the universal Church is realized through the communion of our bishop with his fellow bishops, whose overall unity is visibly expressed in the primacy of the Bishop of Rome.

This understanding of the Church as communion was enhanced by Chapter Seven of *Lumen gentium* on 'The Pilgrim Church'. This Church, whose life is communion, is a Church living in history, always recalling the life of her incarnate Lord, especially his death and resurrection, as she looks forward in hope to his coming in glory and the full establishment of his Kingdom. In other words, the communion of the Church on earth is a communion on the way, longing for its completion in the perfect communion of the age to come. 'Beloved, we are God's children now; it does not yet appear what we shall be, but we know that when he appears we shall be like him, for we shall see him as he is' (1 John 3:2). This eschatological aspect of the Church and her communion will later be more fully developed in the *Catechism of the Catholic Church*.

So the Church is in her deepest reality communion: communion in Christ, communion with Christ, the communication of Christ. The other more institutional aspects of the Church - diocesan structures, parishes and religious congregations; liturgical rites, theology, and canon law - exist in their different ways to promote and protect this profound reality of communion. Ultimately, they have no other purpose.

Areas of Application

This understanding of the Church as communion has vital consequences for our understanding of all church life.

Authority. First, it affects our understanding of authority. While the authority of Pope and bishops is naturally upheld, it is now placed in a broader and deeper context. The Church's ministry exists as a service to this communion in the Spirit. The communion that is the Church is a structured communion, with the ordained ministry as a structuring instrument for the formation of communion in Christ. The diocese is 'formed by him [the bishop] into one community in the Holy Spirit through the Gospel and the Eucharist' (*Christus dominus*, para. 11).

Collegiality of the Bishops. The teaching of *Lumen gentium* on the collegiality of the bishops emphasizes the aspect of communion inherent in the ministry of Pope and bishops. Thus, 'the Bishop of Rome...is the supreme visible bond of the communion of the particular Churches in the one Church and the guarantor of their freedom' (CCC, para. 1559). This aspect of communion is expressed in all inter-diocesan synods, whether provincial, national or international, and at the ordination of a new bishop in the requirement that there be at least three consecrating bishops.

Laity. The vision of the Church as communion also provides the deepest ground for a full honouring of all the laity as active members of the Church. Once we grasp that all Christians, ordained and unordained, are sharers in this Trinitarian communion, drawn into the missions of the Son and the Spirit, it is no longer possible to regard the real differences between clergy and laity as more important than what we share as fellow Christians. The focus on communion as the heart of the Church gives full weight to the leading and the inspiration of the Holy Spirit, who cannot be programmed or controlled.

Ecumenism. The Church as communion also provides the only adequate framework for an understanding of ecumenism, for all relationships between the Catholic Church and other Christian Churches and communities. Before Vatican II, the Church meant the Catholic Church, and other Christians were simply seen as 'outside the Church'. Unfortunately this often remains the way that Catholics speak. But in the theology of communion, other Christian bodies and their members are not 'outside': they are 'inside the mystery of the Church'. Communion is not an all or nothing concept. Communion admits of degrees. So, in fact, the Council documents speak of other Christians as being in 'real, but imperfect communion' with the Catholic Church.[5]

Mary. Communion and its eschatological fulfilment also enable us to situate the unique place of Mary in the Church and the Christian life. During the Council, Paul VI declared that Mary is 'the mother of the Church'. This title brings out the relationship of the mother of the Lord to all believers. In fact, what some Catholics seek to express by calling Mary 'the mediatrix of all graces' is far better expressed in the title 'mother of the Church'. Everything positive about Mary's role within the Body of Christ is captured by her role as mother, for everything about a mother is deeply personal and relational. The terminology of 'graces' can too easily reflect an external and impersonal view of Mary as a dispenser of spiritual commodities.

The Eastern Church has always preserved an understanding of the Church as communion. This can be seen in the place of the Eucharist in the Orthodox theology of the Church. It can also be seen in the design of an Orthodox church building, in which the icons reflect a picture of the heavenly Church in which the saints are united in perfect communion. The congregation gathers on earth to worship in the fellowship of this great 'cloud of witnesses' (Heb. 12:1). In this communion, Jesus stands at the centre, the Pantocrator, the Lord of all and head of the Body. Then Mary has her key place on the icon screen before the sanctuary, offering her Son to the world.

Liturgy and Eucharist

These developments in Catholic ecclesiology were themselves facilitated by the Council's treatment of the liturgy before the theme of the Church. Already in the Constitution on the Liturgy, it was stated that 'the liturgy is the summit towards which the activity of the Church is directed; it is also the fount from which all her power flows' (SC, para. 10). The same paragraph then makes plain the central place of the Eucharist in the Church's liturgy. The more we understand the Church as communion, the more central the Eucharist becomes as the sacrament of communion between God and humankind in Christ Jesus. More than any other aspect of the life of the Church, the Eucharist foreshadows and prepares us for the full and total communion of the coming Kingdom.

Notes

[1] In the twentieth century, the great pioneers of a renewed Catholic theology of the Church were Karl Adam (1876–1966), Emile Mersch (1890–1940) and Yves Congar (1904–95). In a less academic way, the writings of the Abbot of Buckfast, Dom Anscar Vonier (1875–1938), also made a valuable contribution.

[2] E.g. the documents on bishops, on priests, on priestly formation, on the lay apostolate, on religious life, on the missionary work of the Church, on ecumenism, on non-Christian religions.

[3] F. Blachnicki, 'Aspetti caratterizzanti un movimento

ecclesiale' in *I Movimenti nella Chiesa*, ed. M. Camisasca and M. Vitali (Milan: Jaca, 1982), p. 177.

[4] The local church is sometimes called a 'particular Church' in the Council documents.

[5] The Decree on Ecumenism, para. 3, formulates more explicitly what was first sketched in *Lumen gentium,* para. 15.

Church *Forward*

PART II

Church *Forward*

PROLOGUE

Part I reflected on the contribution of Pope John XXIII and the Second Vatican Council to the renewal of the Catholic Church. Part II will look at some key developments in the forty years since the end of the Council. The next four chapters (Nine to Twelve) examine developments that almost certainly could not have happened without the Council, but which go beyond the implementation of the Council's decisions and what was imagined in 1965.

These four developments - on evangelization, solidarity, repentance for the sins of the past and the new ecclesial movements - were none of them mandated by the Council. But they are all developments within the logic of the Council. They can rightly be seen as fruits of the Council, even though not foreseen fruits. We can understand each of them as a work of the Holy Spirit building on the Spirit's work at the Council. These four topics have been singled out for specific mention because of their relationship to the renewal of the Church. They are each given a chapter because each contributes to the Church's renewal something fundamental and irreplaceable.

Chapter Thirteen provides a reflection on the distinctive contribution of Pope John Paul II to the renewal of the Church. This contribution which flows directly from the personal experience and gifts of the late Pope could obviously not have been foreseen before his election. Because this chapter deals with the synthesis of Catholic teaching effected by John Paul II, it inevitably brings together many elements mentioned in earlier chapters. John Paul II himself saw his contribution in the context of the full implementation of the vision of the Council.

Chapter Fourteen is somewhat different. It also looks at developments in the post-conciliar period, but it raises the question of uncompleted business and of what is needed to carry forward the renewal of the Church, particularly in terms of ecumenical relations and sharing.

CHAPTER NINE
Evangelization

The renewal of Catholic life requires an explicit proclamation of the gospel of salvation. Renewal has to start with renewal of faith, and faith comes by hearing the Word. The need for this evangelization or initial proclamation is now recognized in official church documents.

Evangelization is a new word in everyday Catholic terminology. It is a fruit of the Council. Although the word was little used in the Council documents,[1] a new focus on evangelization was totally within the logic of the Council. First, the new attention given to the Scriptures led to a new focus on the proclamation of the Word of God, and so to explicit evangelization. Second, it is wholly consonant with the emphasis placed on the active role of the laity in the life of the Church. So when *Lumen gentium* speaks of the laity sharing in the priestly, kingly and prophetic roles of Christ, it is under their prophetic role that mention is made of evangelization, which is 'the proclamation of Christ by word and the testimony of life' (para. 35). Third, the Council's decision to restore the adult catechumenate inevitably required attention to be given to the first steps in coming to the faith and the criteria for the admission of candidates as catechumens.[2]

The first of these factors is the most basic. The new emphasis on the Bible makes the Word of God central to the renewal of the Church. In effect, it requires the formulation of a Catholic theology of the Word of God. For it is by the preached Word that people are brought to faith and to conversion. 'Faith comes from what is heard, and what is heard comes by the preaching of Christ' (Rom. 10:17). The Council's theology of Divine Revelation reminds us that Christian faith is not belief in a theory, however intelligently formulated, but is faith in a God who has spoken in human history. 'In many and various ways God spoke of old to our fathers by the prophets; but in these last days he has spoken to us by a Son, whom he appointed the heir of all things, through whom also he created the world' (Heb. 1:1-2). That is why for Christians faith is not produced by reflection alone, but is a response to the proclamation of the words and acts of God.

Evangelii Nuntiandi

The entry of the term 'evangelization' into regular Catholic discourse came through Paul VI's Apostolic Letter *Evangelii nuntiandi*, issued in 1975, following the Synod of Bishops on Evangelization in 1974. The importance of *Evangelii nuntiandi* lies first in the Pope's insistence on the necessity of proclaiming the Good News of the gospel. Perhaps in reaction to Evangelical Protestant patterns of explicit evangelism, Catholics have often defended a meagre spoken witness by an insistence on the witness of a holy life. Paul VI directly addressed this when he wrote: 'The Good News proclaimed by the witness of life sooner or later has to be proclaimed by the word of life. There is no true evangelization if the name, the teaching, the life, the promises, the Kingdom and the mystery of Jesus of Nazareth, the Son of God are not proclaimed' (EN, para. 22).

In fact, *Evangelii nuntiandi* is primarily about proclamation. The first part is entitled: 'From Christ the Evangelizer to the Evangelizing Church'. Jesus is the first Evangelizer. 'Evangelizing is in fact the grace and vocation proper to the Church, her deepest identity' (para. 14). Proclaiming the gospel is not just one of the things the Church does; it belongs to her essence. Evangelization is central to the renewal of the Church.

In a section on 'The Content of Evangelization', Paul VI recognizes that there is an 'essential content, the living substance' that cannot be omitted (EN, para. 25). Here the Pope begins this task of identifying the core message to be proclaimed. He describes as 'the foundation, centre and... summit of its dynamism... a clear proclamation that, in Jesus Christ, the Son of God, made man, who died and rose from the dead, salvation is offered to all men, as a gift of God's grace and mercy' (EN, para. 27). Here we can see a key recognition of the essential distinction between the initial proclamation of the gospel to those without faith and the beginnings of systematic teaching to believers in catechesis. This distinction is of huge significance for the renewal of the Church, for it represents a rediscovery of the conversion-provoking and life-giving character of gospel proclamation.

Also very important in *Evangelii nuntiandi* is the Pope's teaching on the role of the Holy Spirit. Here the link between evangelization and renewal is evident. Although this teaching comes near the end of the document, it is a powerful word that should not be forgotten. 'Evangelization will never be possible without the action of the Holy Spirit.' And then: 'the Holy Spirit is the principal agent of evangelization' (EN, para. 75). We can say that this opening of the Catholic Church to explicit evangelization is a *kairos* from the Lord, for Paul VI recognizes that 'we live in the Church at a privileged moment of the Spirit' (EN, para. 75).[3]

Tensions and Challenges

It is not surprising that this re-thinking of the Church's apostolate should pose deep challenges both to Catholic practice and to Catholic theology. In the thirty years since *Evangelii nuntiandi,* we can see both the pastoral ministry and the magisterium of the Church grappling with these issues. In the teaching of the magisterium, besides the new *Rite of Christian Initiation for Adults* (RCIA), issued in 1972 and *Evangelii nuntiandi*, there is important teaching in the letters of John Paul II: *Catechesi tradendae* (1983) on catechesis, and *Redemptoris missio* (1986) on the mission of the Church. Much of this is brought together in greater detail in the *General Directory on Catechesis* (GDC, 1997). We can summarize the key issues regarding evangelization in this way: (a) the proper terminology; (b) what is the basic gospel? (c) event versus process; (d) the relationship between person and community/society.

(a) The Proper Terminology. In RCIA, the term 'evangelization' refers to the first of three phases in the process of Christian initiation.[4] It refers to the period of proclamation of the basic gospel message. In the later documents, particularly in GDC, it is called 'initial' or 'primary proclamation', and the term 'Evangelization' refers to all stages of Christian initiation and formation throughout life. However, in much popular usage, it would seem that

evangelization is still being used in the RCIA and *Evangelii nuntiandi* sense of explicit proclamation. While the teaching but not the terminology of the GDC is the same, it would seem that, if evangelization is to be used in the more global GDC sense, then a less clumsy designation is needed for the 'initial' or 'primary' proclamation.

(b) What Is the Basic Gospel? On the one hand, the Catholic documents since Vatican II clearly recognize that there is an initial message to be proclaimed that is different from systematic catechesis. The use of the term 'proclamation' recognizes that there is an event to be announced, something decisive that has happened. This event is the incarnation of the Son of God, that culminates in his death on the cross and his resurrection from the dead.[5] It is the proclamation of this event that elicits faith and conversion. On the other hand, there is a difficulty in saying what belongs to this 'initial proclamation' and what does not. Is the proclamation simply of the death and resurrection of Jesus, or of his whole life and teaching?[6] As the proclamation is widened beyond the actual events of the life of Jesus, does the initial proclamation start to slide into the systematic teaching of catechesis with a consequent loss of evangelistic impact?

These questions are unavoidable as the Catholic Church with its traditional concern for teaching the fullness of Catholic doctrine addresses the breakdown in the system of initiating children and youth into the faith of the Church. The traditional system of presenting the whole Catholic faith from an early age is no longer working. In Europe, the leakage rate of children educated in Catholic schools is enormous. In many countries, the majority of children in Catholic secondary schools are no longer attending Mass on Sundays. The systematic teaching of the faith even seems to have the effect of inoculating them against faith rather than instilling and strengthening faith. In this age of widespread dechristianization, presenting the whole Catholic faith without initial proclamation does not bring people to conversion.[7]

Moreover, as we shall see when we look at the new ecclesial movements in the contemporary Church, the proclamation of a basic gospel message is effective, even in a highly secularized society. Nonetheless, while the need for a basic proclamation of Jesus Christ is clearly stated in the documents of the magisterium, it is still insufficiently understood at many levels of the Church. This misunderstanding is most obvious where RCIA is used as a form of 'evangelization' (in Paul VI's sense), rather than as the catechesis needed to lead the newly evangelized to full participation in the life of the Church.

(c) Event versus Process. The focus on event, both the event of Jesus Christ and the event of conversion, introduces a new tension into Catholic reflection and debate. Catholics have long thought in terms of process, whether the process of

church tradition through history or the process of sanctification throughout life. But the entry of the Word into the picture introduces the element of event, for the spoken and preached Word is always event.

The admission of an element of event has obvious consequences for our understanding of conversion. Thus, the purpose of initial proclamation is to produce an initial conversion.[8] The instructions for RCIA make plain that only those who show signs of an initial conversion are to be admitted as catechumens.[9] However, this event-character of initial conversion then begins the process of ongoing and deepening conversion. As the New Testament indicates,[10] initial conversion is like birth at the beginning of the process of life: 'Adhering to Jesus Christ... sets in motion a process of continuing conversion' (GDC, para. 56). However, the GDC distinguishes between the process of conversion during the catechumenate leading to 'mature faith' and the ongoing conversion required of the mature Christian after the completion of pre-baptismal and post-baptismal catechesis.[11] In some way, this parallels the process of childhood issuing in the process that is the life of an adult.

The change in terminology from 'evangelization' (pre-catechumenate) to 'initial' or 'primary proclamation' is clearly motivated by awareness that the proclamation of the Word and the need for conversion continue throughout life. This is why in the GDC, 'Evangelization' becomes the overarching word to describe the evangelistic and formative work of the Church through all stages of life. The process of evangelization comprises: 'Christian witness, dialogue and presence in charity, the proclamation of the Gospel and the call to conversion, the catechumenate and Christian Initiation, the formation of the Christian communities through and by means of the sacraments and their ministers' (GDC, para. 47).

Maybe we should expect further developments in Catholic understanding of conversion as event and process. Much of the GDC content is optimum theory put together by experts and specialists rather than a reflection of what is actually happening in most parishes. The Catholic experience of initial proclamation of the basic Christ-event is quite recent, but expanding. Despite official documents, there is much popular Catholic resistance to any idea of identifiable moments of conversion, felt by many to be typically Evangelical Protestant. But, in fact, the event-character of conversion is a direct consequence of the event-character of the preached Word. As Catholic preaching becomes more biblical, and as there is more Catholic proclamation of the basic gospel, we should expect a greater recognition of conversion as an event, not only as a one-off event, but as an event beginning a new process.

(d) Person and Community/Society. Another tension linked to the issue of event and process is the tension between the individual person and the community or society.

Just as Catholics have emphasized process, so have we emphasized the place of each person in society and in community, in the Church and in the world. When there is a focus on personal conversion, Catholics are often worried about imbibing an individualistic model from Evangelical Protestant sources.

The Catholic concern to situate the Christian in Church and the person in society has taken two main forms. The first is to insist that the task of evangelization is an ecclesial task. Paul VI said that 'there is a profound link between Christ, the Church and evangelization' (EN, para. 16). Evangelization is an activity of the Church. The message proclaimed is the gospel entrusted to the Church.[12] RCIA illustrates this ecclesial context: all stages of Christian initiation involve a ministry of the Church bringing new life to birth and to maturity within the Church.

The second Catholic concern is that the object of evangelization should not be understood in an individualistic way. Persons belong to families, clans or tribes, villages, towns and cities, nations and cultures. Thus, Paul VI wrote, 'Evangelization would not be complete if it did not take account of the unceasing interplay of the gospel and of man's concrete life, both personal and social' (EN, para. 29). As a consequence, the task of evangelization has to flow out from the conversion of persons to the evangelization of culture. Paul VI observed that 'the split between the Gospel and culture is without a doubt the drama of our time' (EN, para.

20). 'Therefore every effort must be made to ensure a full evangelization of culture, or, more correctly, of cultures. They have to be regenerated by an encounter with the Gospel. But this encounter will not take place if the Gospel is not proclaimed' (EN, para. 20).[13]

The fear of the protagonists of conversion is that efforts to influence society will fail if there is not a proclamation leading to conversion. The fear of the protagonists of social and cultural renewal is that a focus on individual conversions can overlook the social dimension of conversion, and ultimately produce inauthentic Christians, whose public lives do not correspond to their personal profession. The answer cannot lie in being dominated by these fears. The renewal of the Church requires an evangelization that impacts people in all the dimensions of their lives: private, familial, public, social, economic and cultural. Here again we must remember that explicit proclamation of the Jesus-event is a new development in Catholic life, and we are only at the beginning of seeing the fruits. Some of these will be mentioned in a later chapter on new ecclesial movements.[14]

Notes

[1] The term 'evangelization' occurs a few times in *Apostolicam actuositatem*, the Decree on the Apostolate of Lay People and in *Ad gentes,* the Decree on the Missionary Activity of the Church. The latter uses the term more than the former (see paras. 6, 14, 23, 30, 38, 39 and 41), but most of these references are to the missionary expansion of the

Church through the ministry of missionaries and catechists. In the former decree, the apostolate of the laity is exercised 'when they work at the evangelization and sanctification of men' (AA, para. 2), but the category of apostolate is all-pervasive and 'evangelization' is not the focus. Perhaps the Council's most important statement on this subject comes when it is said that 'the whole church is missionary, and the work of evangelization [is] the fundamental task of the people of God' (AG, para. 35).

[2] 'The catechumenate for adults, comprising several distinct steps, is to be restored and brought into use at the discretion of the local ordinary [bishop]' (SC, para. 64).

[3] This statement comes a few months after the Holy Father had welcomed the Catholic charismatic renewal to Rome with the statement that it represents a 'chance for the Church'.

[4] The other two phases are Catechesis (the period from enrolment in the catechumenate through to baptism) and Mystagogia (the immediate post-baptismal formation).

[5] 'The subject of proclamation is Christ who was crucified, died and is risen: through him is accomplished our full and authentic liberation from evil, sin and death; through him God bestows "new life" that is divine and eternal. This is the "Good News" which changes man and his history, and which all peoples have a right to hear' (John Paul II, *Redemptoris missio,* para. 44).

[6] Compare the citations of Paul VI above from paragraphs 22 and 27 of *Evangelii nuntiandi*.

[7] If we ask why this method did better in the past, the short answer is 'Mothers'; a longer answer would point to the strength of family life, the formative role of both parents and the support of the enveloping culture.

[8] 'Primary proclamation is addressed to non-believers and those living in religious indifference. Its functions are to proclaim the Gospel and to call for conversion' (GDC, para.

61; cf. also paras. 48 and 88).

[9] 'There must be evidence of the first faith that was conceived during the period of evangelization and precatechumenate and of an initial conversion and intention to change their lives and to enter into a relationship with God in Christ' (RCIA, para. 42). See also GDC, para. 62.

[10] See, for example, 1 Peter 1:23.

[11] See GDC, paras. 56d, 67.

[12] This is true of all stages in evangelization: see GDC, paras. 43, 78-79, 105-106.

[13] In relation to catechesis and culture, see GDC, paras. 109-110, 202-204.

[14] See Chapter Twelve.

Church *Forward*

CHAPTER TEN
Solidarity

Solidarity is the free bonding of responsible people for the common good. It is an outworking of communion in society. The renewal of the Church requires the solidarity of Christians realizing the unity of the Body of Christ in service to the world. The Eucharist is a summons to solidarity.

In Part I, we looked at the new attention to the dignity of the human person in the Vatican II documents,[1] and then at the emerging understanding of the Church as communion.[2] We turn now to another aspect of renewal that has emerged since Vatican II, which is an application of these themes to the renewal of society. This is the concept of solidarity, which is a realization of truly human association for the good of the community and society.

Solidarity in Recent Times

Many people heard the term 'solidarity' for the first time during the struggle of the Polish workers against Communism in the late 1970s. When groups of Polish workers took the bold step in a Communist nation of forming a trade union, they called their movement *Solidarnosc*, the Polish word for solidarity. We may remember televised scenes from the shipyards of Danzig, a Solidarity stronghold under the leadership of Lech Walesa, where workers resisted government attempts to shut down the trade union. This uprising of the workers was a double blow against the Communist system. Not only was a section of the public protesting against the system, but the protest came from the workers who in the official ideology were the great beneficiaries of the Marxist vision.

Did the decision to call this trade union in Poland by the name of 'Solidarity' have anything to do with Catholic teaching? Yes, because the workers who formed the Solidarity trade union had been strongly influenced by the Oasis retreat movement, founded in Poland by Fr Franciszek Blachnicki, who was in close touch with the then Mgr Wojtyla.[3] The Solidarity trade union embodied the personalist vision of Archbishop Wojtyla. This is one reason why the struggles between Solidarity and the Communist government never led to violent confrontation. When

Cardinal Wojtyla became Pope, the concept of solidarity was an intrinsic element in his teaching on the dignity of the human person. Some years later, John Paul II reflected: 'It cannot be forgotten that the fundamental crisis of systems claiming to express the rule and indeed the dictatorship of the working class began with the great upheavals which took place in Poland in the name of solidarity' (CA, para. 23). Thus, for the Pope, solidarity was not just the name of a trade union, but expressed a corporate response arising from the conscientious convictions of a Christian people. Outside Poland, there was a solidarity among the people in several nations of Eastern Europe as the Communist system collapsed. The particular character of solidarity is seen in the influence of profound convictions and moral principles upon whole peoples, leading to the overthrow of a tyrannical system without violence.[4]

Other examples of solidarity at the level of national populations in modern times can be seen in the massive but peaceful protest of the Filipino people against the Marcos regime, which led to its overthrow and to the presidency of Cory Aquino. Most recently, in December 2004, the protest of the Ukrainian people against a fraudulent election, again with a remarkable absence of violence, can be seen as another instance of solidarity.

How Did Solidarity Enter into Catholic Teaching?

The term 'solidarity' can hardly be regarded as part of the terminology of the Second Vatican Council. In the Council documents, it is Part I of *Gaudium et spes* that develops most fully the Catholic understanding of human beings in society, but the term 'solidarity' only occurs in paragraph 32, both in the heading 'The Word Made Flesh and Human Solidarity' and in the final sentence, where, interestingly, it is applied to the Church.

Pope Paul VI had mentioned 'the duty of human solidarity' in his letter *Populorum progressio* (1967). However, here the term has not yet acquired the richness of meaning that it will receive from Pope John Paul II. For Paul VI this meant 'the aid that the rich nations must give to developing countries' (PP, paras. 44, 48). On the three duties of human solidarity, of social justice and of universal charity 'depends the future of the civilization of the world' (PP, para. 44).[5]

It is with Pope John Paul II that the term 'solidarity' takes on a specific and consistent meaning in Catholic social teaching. His understanding of solidarity is rooted in his understanding of the human person. The origins of this reflection on the human person go back to the Pope's doctoral studies on the German philosopher Max Scheler (1874-1928) and to a group of philosophers at the Catholic University of

Lublin in the late 1940s and the early 1950s. The young Fr Karol Wojtyla formed part of this group. These men had shared the experience of Nazi oppression during World War II, and were now living under Communist and Soviet domination. They were convinced that the devastating tyrannies of Nazism and Communism flowed from a false understanding of society and the human person. They saw that the neo-scholastic philosophy that had long reigned in Catholic thinking was not adequate to the challenge. Unlike scholasticism, which began from the natures and essences of things, they began from a detailed study of human experience in all its richness. As they undertook this study, they were aware of its crucial importance for the future of human society. If they could establish a convincing account of the human person from an examination of human experience, not just individual experience but also human experience in society, then this could effect a reconciliation between Catholic philosophy and the sciences, particularly the social and behavioural sciences, while avoiding the dangers of all a priori systems and ideologies.

Later, as a bishop deeply involved in the production of *Gaudium et spes*,[6] Mgr Wojtyla was acutely aware of the need for a deep philosophical underpinning of the Council's teaching on the dignity of the human person. Out of this concern came his book *Osoba y czyn* (Person and Act).[7] For Wojtyla, each of us grows as a person through our exercise of intelligence, of choice and of decision, thus realizing our freedom through conforming it to what is good and true. It is in moral action that the human person integrates the different levels of the spirit, the mind and the body. But his book is not just about the acts of individuals, but the acts of persons in society. The key question becomes: How should human persons act together? It is here that the distinctive concept of human solidarity appears.

Once Cardinal Wojtyla becomes Pope, solidarity enters into official Catholic teaching in a more precise way. For John Paul II, solidarity is the virtue that holds human society together. The unity of human society cannot be something imposed from the outside, but arises from the free choice of responsible persons acting in freedom. His first encyclical, *Redemptor hominis* (1979), speaks of 'the principle of solidarity'. The Pope speaks of the need to transform 'the structures of economic life' and says: 'The task requires resolute commitment by individuals and peoples that are free and linked in solidarity' (RH, para. 16). Solidarity is the free bonding of people for the common good.

Obviously with his insider knowledge of the struggle of the Polish workers against the Communist system, John Paul II saw one obvious area for the practice of solidarity to be the workplace. So in his encyclical letter *Laborem exercens* (1981), there is a heading 'Worker Solidarity' (para. 8). But here in fact the Pope is summarizing the contributions of past Popes, especially Leo XIII, to the understanding of workers' rights, and he interprets their recommendations as urging solidarity, although they did not use this term.

Another reference to solidarity occurs in the Pope's letter *Familiaris consortio* on family life, also issued in 1981. He sees the family as 'the first and irreplaceable school of social life'. It is in the family that the child learns the law of 'free-giving' in the form of 'heartfelt acceptance, encounter and dialogue, disinterested availability, generous service and deep solidarity' (FC, para. 43).

In the encyclical *Sollicitudo rei socialis* (1987), John Paul II speaks of solidarity as 'interdependence', especially in paragraphs 38-40. The 'structures of sin' that so shape our world, often based on human greed and the thirst for power, can only be overcome 'by a diametrically opposed attitude: a commitment to the good of one's neighbour with the readiness, in the gospel sense, to "lose oneself" for the sake of the other instead of exploiting him, and to "serve him" instead of oppressing him for one's own advantage (cf. Matt. 10:40-42; 20:25; Mark 10:42-45; Luke 22:25-27)' (SRS, para. 38). This willingness to serve alongside others is solidarity.

Solidarity is based upon mutual recognition as human persons (SRS, para. 39). Solidarity means seeing the other, 'whether a person, people or nation not just as some kind of instrument, with a work capacity and physical strength to be exploited at low cost and then discarded when no longer useful, but as our "neighbour", a "helper" to be made a sharer, on a par with ourselves, in the banquet of life to which all are equally invited by God' (SRS, para. 39).

In 1991, soon after the collapse of Soviet-style Communism, John Paul II reflected in his encyclical *Centesimus annus* on the end of the cold war. He first notes the merely materialistic ways in which the West fought Communism: either by 'national security', so controlling the whole of society in order to make Marxist infiltration impossible, or in the 'affluent society or the consumer society' to defeat Marxism on the level of pure materialism (CA, para. 19). Either way, the dignity of the human person suffered at the hands of political control or of economic greed. But then the Pope reflects on how Communism was actually overthrown: in the collapse of Communism, almost entirely without violence, the victory of freedom over political and military might was only possible through the virtue of solidarity: 'the fall of this kind of "bloc" or empire was accomplished almost everywhere by means of peaceful protest, using only the weapons of truth and justice' (CA, para. 23).

The Urgent Need for Solidarity Today

In the world today it seems that many nations are becoming more fearful and self-protective. It is easy for political leaders, who have to face re-election every few years, to pay more attention to opinion polls than to the needs of poorer nations and the requirements of international justice. As the world becomes more unstable, an instability itself fuelled by flagrant injustice, people are less willing to make sacrifices for the sake of justice and the well-being of the most oppressed. Here the Pope's call for the practice of the virtue of solidarity is a cry to break out of this vicious circle of self-protection and mistrust. Either we practise solidarity or we risk world catastrophe.

It is no accident that this teaching on human solidarity as a virtue developed under Communist tyranny. For it is an assertion of the inter-connectedness of all human beings, but in a Christian framework that insists on human freedom and human dignity. The Communist philosophy saw the need for protection from individual greed, but its collectivist solution sacrificed human dignity and personal liberty. In the days of Soviet Communism, the fear of Communist revolution helped to restrain the excesses of a capitalism that promotes the freedom of the powerful at the expense of human togetherness.

The sphere of ecology and global warming is one of the areas where human solidarity alone can avert disaster. It requires concerted action by the nations acting together for the good of the whole world, i.e., solidarity. But democratic governments are paralysed by their fear of rejection by the voters and by the pressures of major commercial interests. As long as the voters are locked into a self-centred pursuit of their own personal goals and desires and do not grasp the effectiveness of truly corporate action, nothing significant will happen at government level. Solidarity is 'people power' exercised in a responsible way that is respectful of human freedom and dignity.

Solidarity expresses the commitment to human society and culture, that is to 'the common good', but rooted in a deep respect for the value and the dignity of each human being. Solidarity recognizes the transcendence of the human being, whose heart can never be satisfied with material possessions alone: 'there are collective and qualitative needs which cannot be satisfied by market mechanisms. There are important human needs which escape its logic. There are goods which by their very nature cannot and must not be bought or sold' (CA, para. 40).

Solidarity as a Fruit of the Council

In retrospect, we can see that the emergence of solidarity as a key concept in the Catholic understanding of society is a direct fruit of the Council. It is a consequence of the teaching on the dignity of the human person, with its emphasis on both the social context of all human life and the freedom that marks human dignity. We need not only terminology to describe the human person and the various components in human dignity, but also a word to describe what this teaching produces when it is acted upon and realized in society. That word is solidarity.

Solidarity can thus be seen as a necessary accompaniment of communion. Maybe we can say that solidarity in society is the equivalent of communion in the Church. The Pope's insight into the role of the family as the first school of solidarity also points to this link between solidarity and communion. This link indicates the importance of the Eucharist for the formation of solidarity. In the Church this astonishing mixture of people from all races, languages and nations is formed into one body through the gift of the one body. 'Because there is one bread, we who are many are one body, for we all partake of the one bread' (1 Cor. 10:17).

John Paul II took up this theme of the Eucharist and solidarity at the end of his Apostolic Letter *Mane nobiscum domine* (2004), introducing the Year of the Eucharist:

> The Eucharist is not merely an expression of communion in the Church's life; it is also a project of solidarity for all of humanity. In the celebration of the Eucharist the Church constantly renews her awareness of being a "sign and instrument" not only of intimate union with God but also of the unity of the whole human race. Each Mass, even when celebrated in obscurity or in isolation, always has a universal character. The Christian who takes part in the Eucharist learns to become a *promotor of communion, peace and solidarity* in every situation. More than ever, our troubled world, which began the new Millennium with

the spectre of terrorism and the tragedy of war, demands that Christians learn to experience the Eucharist as a *great school of peace,* forming men and women who, at various levels of responsibility in social, cultural and political life, can become promoters of dialogue and communion (para. 27).

However, this vision of the Eucharist as the food of solidarity in human society makes more urgent the healing of the wounds of Christian division. For the Eucharist can only provide the glue for human solidarity, when all Christians can be welcomed at the one Table of the Lord.

Notes

[1] See Chapter Four.
[2] See Chapter Eight.
[3] On the Oasis movement, see Chapter Twelve.
[4] The only place where there was some violence in 1989 was in Romania.
[5] See also PP, paras 17, 84.
[6] Mgr Wojtyla took part in the first two sessions of the Council (1962–63) as an auxiliary Bishop of Cracow, and in the 3rd and 4th sessions (1964–65) as Archbishop. He was a member of the joint commission that worked on the drafts for *Gaudium et spes.*
[7] The English translation of this book is entitled *The Acting Person.* The Pope's biographer, George Weigel, criticizes this translation and the title: see *Witness to Hope (*New York: HarperCollins, 1999), footnote to pp. 174-75.

CHAPTER ELEVEN
Repentance for the Sins of the Past

Repentance for sin is a work of the Holy Spirit. It is the way that the Lord deals with evil in its roots. This is as true for the corporate life of the Church as it is true for each individual. Repentance for the sins of the past is thus an indispensable element in the renewal of the Church.

The need for Catholics to confess the sins of the past with humility and penitence was first made clear by Pope John Paul II in 1994 in his letter *Tertio millennio adveniente,* calling the Catholic Church to prepare for the Great Jubilee of the year 2000. The Church 'cannot cross the threshold of the new millennium without encouraging her children to purify themselves through repentance of past errors and instances of infidelity, inconsistency and slowness to act' (TMA, para. 33).

While this call of the Pope was new and unprecedented, it was wholly in the logic of the Council's Decree on Ecumenism. It can be seen as a further unpacking of the declaration: 'There can be no ecumenism worthy of the name without interior conversion' (UR, para. 7); likewise of the Council's recognition that where there had been negative elements in the life of the Church, 'these should be set right at the opportune time and in the proper way' (UR, para. 6).[1]

In retrospect, it may seem obvious that the Council's call to 'continual reformation' (UR, para. 6) had to lead to a confession of the sins of the past. In fact, it took thirty years for this logical development to take place, because it required not just theological acumen but also spiritual insight allied to the courage of John Paul II. John Paul II first mentioned his plan to issue this call to a meeting of all the cardinals in 1993, and apparently it did not meet with enthusiastic support. But the Holy Father was convinced that he must proceed. He knew in his spirit the necessity of this confession for the renewal of the Church and the healing of the world.

What factors contributed to the Pope's decision? One major element comes from his awareness of the sins of Catholics against the Jewish people. Following the issue of *Tertio millennio adveniente*, the Pope set up special commissions of experts to study the Catholic treatment of the Jewish people throughout the centuries, as well as another on the Church Inquisitions, including the Spanish Inquisition, in whose work the issue of the *conversos*, the baptized Jews, was central.[2] But it is clear that from the start of John Paul II's pontificate he knew that it was his task to lead the Catholic Church into the new millennium. His conviction reflects both his life-long meditation on the major evils of the twentieth century, through which he had himself lived in Poland, and his sense of the year 2000 presenting a historic opportunity for the Church and for the world. In preparing for the new millennium, he sought to 'look with the eyes of faith' (TMA, para. 17) at the whole history of the Church, at the second millennium between the years 1000 and 2000 and very particularly at the twentieth century, 'a century scarred by the First and Second World Wars, by the experience of concentration camps and by horrendous massacres. All these events demonstrate most vividly that the world needs purification; it needs to be converted' (TMA, para. 18).

The result of the Pope's call for a confession of the sins of the past during the celebration of the Great Jubilee was the penitential liturgy celebrated in St Peter's, Rome, on 12 March 2000, and personally presided over by the Pope. In this liturgy, seven prelates from key offices in the Roman Curia confessed the sins of the past relating to the areas of their official responsibilities.

The Purification of Memories

The Holy Father was well aware that his call for a confession of the sins of the past would lead the Church into new and uncharted territory. It seems that it was probably the Pope himself who first articulated the purpose of this confession as 'the purification of memories'. In the document officially convening the Jubilee Year, *Incarnationis mysterium*[3], he identified 'the purification of the memory' as one of the signs of the mercy of God at work in the Jubilee. 'It requires of all an act of courage and of humility to recognize the faults committed by those who have borne and who bear the name of Christian' (IM, para. 11). After speaking of the holiness of the Church, he said that, even though we do not carry personal responsibility for these sins, 'we bear the weight of the mistakes and the faults of those who went before us' (IM, para. 11).

Memory is a central concept in the document of the International Theological Commission on 'The Church and the Faults of the Past', as is indicated in the title *Memory and Reconciliation* (MR).[4] The Commission explains in its Introduction that: 'This purification aims at liberating personal and communal conscience from all forms of resentment and violence that are the legacy of past faults'. It is important to note the interaction between 'personal' and 'communal' memories. In all human strife, the most dangerous memories are the communal, in the way that a people or a nation remembers its conflicts, writes its history, identifies its enemies, justifies its own behaviour. All these communal memories are accompanied and fuelled by personal memories, by the stories of particular families and individuals with their own sufferings and traumas. These memories are then handed down to the following generations, not only in the official histories, but also in popular culture: in songs, in humour, in memorials and in annual days of remembrance with special ceremonies, often with processions. In these memories the sinful element in the conflicts is perpetuated. We glorify 'our heroes', and excuse their atrocities; and we vilify the other side for whom no excuses are made.

A reflection on this process enables us to understand better why there are so many 'trouble spots' in the world where long-standing conflicts keep erupting like active volcanoes. We can think of former Yugoslavia with the conflict between Catholic Croats and Orthodox Serbs (mixed too with the Muslims in Bosnia), of Northern Ireland (Protestant Unionists and Catholic Nationalists), of Rwanda (Hutu and Tutsi), of Sri Lanka (Singhalese and Tamil). Such conflicts can never be healed without a purification of memories; that is to say, without a purification from the bias and the lies in our histories, and cleansing our hearts of the hatred and the rejection of each other.

The Renewal of the Church

What is the connection between this confession of the sins of the past and the renewal of the Church? First, confession and repentance is an intrinsic part of the process of conversion. Without confession and a sorrow for what has been confessed, there can be no deliverance from evil. And without deliverance, there is no healing. The addressing of the sins of the past is thus indispensable for the Church as well as for the nations and society. But here the Church and the world are not in the same situation. The Church as the herald of the gospel of salvation and as the community called to be a sign of the Kingdom requires purification not just for her own sake but so that she can fulfil her God-given calling in the world. For this reason, the purification of memories within the Church is an essential element in her renewal.

We can start to unpack what this might mean in practice by noting the areas which John Paul II identified as particularly requiring this confession of past sins. These are the areas first of unity,[5] and then intolerance and violence.[6]

The Unity of the Church. We have already noted in Part I on the contribution of Vatican II to renewal that the call to Christian unity is an essential component of church renewal.[7] As has been mentioned, the call to repentance for the sins of the past was not explicitly made in the Council's Decree on Ecumenism, but the seeds are clearly there. As the Decree on Ecumenism came to be implemented in the life of the Catholic Church, more attention was paid to the recommendations concerning theological dialogue and practical collaboration than to the section on 'spiritual ecumenism'. John Paul II once again placed the focus on spiritual ecumenism in his encyclical letter *Ut unum sint* (1995). Not only did the Pope give a major place to joint prayer for unity,[8] he broke new ground by speaking of ecumenical dialogue as an 'examination of conscience'. Referring to 1 John 1:10, he said: 'Such a radical exhortation to acknowledge our condition as sinners ought also to mark the spirit which we bring to ecumenical dialogue' (UUS, para. 34).

John Paul II presented a challenge to the ecumenical movement and to all ecumenists. For what he described as 'the spirit which we bring to ecumenical dialogue' is not in fact a description of how official ecumenical dialogues had been conducted over the previous thirty years. The methods generally followed in the inter-church dialogues were fairly accurately described when the Holy Father explained the limitations of the curent level of dialogue: 'Dialogue cannot take place merely on a horizontal level, being restricted to meetings, exchanges of points of view or even the sharing of gifts proper to each community' (UUS, para. 35). He outlined his own understanding of dialogue: 'It also has a primarily vertical thrust, directed towards the one who, as the Redeemer of the world and the Lord of history, is himself our reconciliation' (UUS, para. 35). This linking of the spiritual and the theological can have revolutionary implications for inter-church relations. It contains the answer to the widespread malaise and disappointment over the slowness of the Churches to receive the fruits of the theological dialogues. It is interesting to note that the Catholic-

Mennonite dialogue, the only bilateral dialogue involving the Catholic Church to have started after *Ut unum sint,* has begun its work with the issue of a Catholic repentance for the persecution of the first Mennonites.

Let us look for a moment at relations between the Catholic Church and the Orthodox Churches. The two major theological issues are the *Filioque*, the phrase in the Latin Credo stating that the Holy Spirit proceeds from the Son as well as from the Father, and the papacy, particularly the Pope's claim to a universal jurisdiction. How might a Catholic confession of the sins of the past affect these theological barriers? The Orthodox-Catholic dialogue in the United States has recently published a report on the issue of the *Filioque*; its final recommendation is that 'the Catholic Church, in the light of a growing theological consensus, and in particular following words of Paul VI, declares that the condemnation of the Second Council of Lyon (1274) of those "who had the audacity to deny that the Holy Spirit proceeds eternally from the Father and the Son" is no longer applicable.'[9] We should notice that this dialogue is operating at the horizontal level: its recommendation is disciplinary and canonical. An act of repentance, dealing with this episode at the Second Council of Lyon, would need to include the vertical level, and become a confession before God of the objective sin involved in this anathematization of fellow Christians.

In fact, John Paul II took several unprecedented steps in Catholic relations with the Orthodox. On more than one occasion, he had the Nicene-Constantinopolitan Creed recited in its original form without the *Filioque,* thus demonstrating at the least that the original and Orthodox confession is still acceptable.[10] He also spoke several times of the Church breathing with 'two lungs', clearly referring to the Eastern and the Western Churches, expressed today especially in the Orthodox and the Catholic Churches. The image of the 'two lungs' has an implicit reference to the Holy Spirit because the Spirit is the breath of God who becomes the breath of the Church. But this suggestive image has not yet provided the basis for an examination of conscience as to how each lung has treated the other.

It is here that one has to move beyond the sphere of doctrine and theology to the actual behaviour of the Churches, their leaders and people. In fact, virtually all specialists in this area insist that a major factor in the Catholic-Orthodox division is the history of Western aggression. The catastrophic event of the sack of Constantinople by the Crusaders in the year 1204 looms large in the Orthodox consciousness. The Crusaders, who were on the way to Jerusalem to liberate the Holy Land from the Muslims, attacked their fellow Christians in Constantinople and looted their treasures. The hurt from this wound was evident when John Paul II visited Athens in 2001, and the Archbishop of Athens, Mgr Christodoulos, directly confronted the Holy Father on this issue. The Pope responded with true humility, did not attempt to justify what happened, and asked for the forgiveness of the Orthodox.

But the wrongs inflicted by the Catholics on the Orthodox did not stop at the violence of the Crusaders. The Patriarchs of the cities of Constantinople, Antioch and Jerusalem were ousted and replaced by Latin Patriarchs; the ancient liturgies of these Churches were replaced by Latin liturgies. Even when these cities came back into Orthodox hands in 1261, Rome still upheld the 'rights' of the imposed Latin patriarchs. The recent Orthodox-Catholic report from the USA refers to this episode in a deliberate understatement: 'This was a clear sign for most Christians in the East that the papacy and its political supporters had little respect for the legitimacy of these ancient Churches.'[11] This is one example of an area where a Catholic confession is still awaited.

The replacement of Eastern hierarchies with Western leads into the issue of 'Uniatism', which the Orthodox regard as the biggest obstacle to dialogue with the Catholic Church. The so-called Uniate Churches, now called in Catholic documents the Eastern Catholic Churches, are those Churches of Eastern tradition in communion with Rome. They are often described in terms of having Eastern liturgical traditions, which is true, but 'being an Eastern Church' involves their whole way of being Christian in liturgy, ethos, theology and spirituality. The Orthodox regard these

Churches as a Western creation to force reluctant Orthodox or to lure unsuspecting Orthodox back into the Roman fold. This is no place to examine the history of the Eastern Catholic Churches, but what needs to be acknowledged is that there is some truth in the Orthodox accusation, though it is not the whole story. The call to repentance means that we have to examine our own house, rather than accuse others. This painful question requires an honest examination by the Catholic Church of this history, leading to a confession of whatever was morally reprehensible, and thus formed part of the sins against 'the unity willed by God for his People'.

Intolerance and Violence. We have seen in these short reflections on the division between the Catholic and the Orthodox Churches that the sins against unity have been closely linked to sins of intolerance and of violence. In considering intolerance and the use of violence in Catholic history, it is appropriate to examine the sins committed against the Jewish people, though this too will lead us back to the sins against unity. The main reason for taking the Jewish people as the prime example here is that the oppression of the Jews at the hands of the Catholic people and authorities has a history that is almost as long as that of the Church. We are not just dealing here with a short-lived phenomenon affecting only one or two generations.

In Chapter Seven, we looked at the Council's repudiation of all anti-Semitism, and in particular at the repudiation of that 'replacement theology' asserting that God had rejected the Jewish people because they had rejected Christ. In this chapter on repentance, it needs to be said that up to this point the Catholic Church has changed the teaching more than it has acknowledged the sin before God. For the assertion that God had rejected the Jews was not just a theological mistake, it was also a sin of judgment, a human usurping of the place of God as judge. Just as sin begets more sin, so this sin of rejecting God's chosen people led to more sin, perhaps first to the sin of contempt and later to that of hatred. It was not surprising then that as soon as the Church had political influence, after the emperors had become Christian, restrictive measures began to be taken against the Jews and the first instances of violence against the Jews are reported. Although the worst oppression of the Jews took place during the second Christian millennium, the seeds for this had been sown in the first millennium. And when there is no repentance, the virus is still alive and ready to strike again.

At the time of the Council, it was recognized that the division between the synagogue and the Church directly touches the unity of the Church. So this also forms part of the sins against 'the unity willed by God for his People'. In fact, the belief that God had rejected the Jews went hand in hand with an exclusion of confessing Jews from the Church. Of course, it was impossible to exclude all Jewish elements from the Church (most importantly, the Church insisted that the Old Testament is inspired Scripture equally with the New

Chapter Eleven • Repentance for the Sins of the Past

Testament), but, by the fourth century, canons were being passed requiring Jewish converts to renounce their Jewish identity and to cease all Jewish practice. Here we can see that the process of repentance, as with all turning away from sin, will itself result in new light, and further layers of sin being uncovered.

The question of the rightness and the necessity of a Jewish expression of the Church is a delicate one for several reasons. Not least, because the Christian behaviour towards the Jewish people has made baptism and conversion a stench in Jewish nostrils. But this issue is unavoidable as the Church today reflects more deeply on Christian sins against the Jewish people. It is also unavoidable because today we have Jewish believers in Jesus claiming that, like the first generation of disciples, they do not cease to be Jews when they believe in Jesus as the Messiah of Israel. Their claim makes us aware in a new way of the appalling agony of conscience experienced by many Jews who came to faith in Jesus over the centuries and were faced with the false choice between hiding or renouncing their new-found faith or embracing Gentile Christianity.

It is not easy to hold together the need to repent for all the oppression of the Jewish people by Christians through the centuries and to repent for the acceptance of the wrong view that one cannot be both a Jew and a believer in Jesus at the same time. We cannot use the claims of Jewish believers in Jesus as an excuse not to listen to the whole Jewish community. There has to be first an acknowledgment of the wrongs done to the Jews and an honouring of them as still the beloved people of the covenant. This also requires a respect for the hesitations and the scepticism of the Jewish people as a whole towards all forms of 'Jewish Christianity'. When the Jewish community sees Jewish believers in Jesus, whether Messianic Jews or Hebrew Catholics, as no longer truly Jewish, this needs to be understood not just as a rejection but as a challenge to address all the wounds of the past.

Here the challenge of repentance for our sins against the Jewish people opens out wider, as is inevitable, to address the extent to which Gentile Christianity has had a distorted understanding of the New Testament, and thus of Jesus, of Mary, of the Twelve, because of reading it through replacement spectacles. In addressing this further challenge, the Jewish believers in Jesus have an indispensable role to play, though a recognized Jewish scholar like the late David Flusser has already made an important contribution to this question. It will inevitably take time for Jewish believers in Jesus to discover what it means to be both Jewish and believers in the Jewish Messiah. We should expect with time that the Jewish believers in Jesus will be more manifestly Jewish in a way that will look different from Gentile Christianity and in a way that their fellow Jews can recognize as Jewish.

Pope John Paul II's call to repentance has opened up - I won't say Pandora's box - it has opened up massive issues that will be part of our agenda for many years. This prospect should not make us fearful, but hopeful, because just as the scope of renewal is greater than we first realized, so the blessings that flow from it will be unimaginably greater.

Notes

[1] The actual wording here in the English translation is: 'if, in various times and circumstances, there have been deficiencies in moral conduct or in Church discipline, or even in the way that Church teaching has been formulated'.

[2] See MR, para. 5.4, pp. 67-69 and the Apostolic Letter *Ecclesia in Europa*, which calls for 'acknowledgment to be given to any part which the children of the Church have had in the growth and spread of antisemitism in history' (para. 56).

[3] Bull dated 29 November 1998.

[4] A preliminary note states that this document was requested by Cardinal Ratzinger (now Pope Benedict XVI). It was published on 7 March 2000, a few days before the celebration of the penitential liturgy in the Vatican.

[5] 'Among the sins which require a greater commitment to repentance and conversion should certainly be counted those which have been detrimental to the unity willed by God for his People' (TMA, para. 34).

[6] 'Another painful chapter of history to which the sons and daughters of the Church must return with a spirit of repentance is that of the acquiescence given, especially in certain centuries, to intolerance and even the use of violence in the service of truth' (TMA, para. 35).

[7] See Chapter Six.

[8] 'Fellowship in prayer leads people to look at the Church and Christianity in a new way' (UUS, para. 23).

[9] Translated from a French version, published in *Irénikon*

LXXVII/1 (2004), p. 100.

[10] This omission occurred first at the celebration of the sixteenth centenary of the Council of Constantinople in 1981, and subsequently on the occasion of visits to Rome by the Patriarchs of Constantinople, Demetrios I in 1987 and Bartholomew I in 1995 and 2004, and of the Romanian Patriarch Theoctist in 2002.

[11] Art. cit., p. 83.

CHAPTER TWELVE
New Ecclesial Movements

Both John Paul II and Benedict XVI have seen the new ecclesial movements in the Catholic Church as a fruit of the Second Vatican Council. They represent an expression of the charismatic dimension of the Church that complements its institutional character. By the way the new movements embody the key emphases of the Council, they represent a significant hope for the future.

The flourishing of new movements in the Catholic Church is one obvious fruit of the Second Vatican Council. In varying degrees, these new movements are characteristic of the era of renewal launched and fostered by the Council. It is true that some movements now recognized as new ecclesial movements were founded before the Council, e.g. the Foyers de Charité, founded in France in 1936, and the Focolari movement, founded in Italy in 1943. But these movements were influenced from the start by the renewal currents in biblical studies, in ecclesiology and in the lay apostolate that came to fruition in the Council. And it is only since the Council that they have become truly international and major influences in the Church.

A key moment in the history of the new ecclesial movements came in May 1998, when Pope John Paul II invited all the new movements and communities to join him for the celebration of Pentecost. On this occasion, the Holy Father spoke about the place of Vatican II in the life of the Catholic Church. The Holy Spirit, he said, 'radically changes people and history. This was the unforgettable experience of the Second Vatican Council, during which, guided by the same Spirit, the Church rediscovered the charismatic dimension as being essential to her identity.' For the Pope, the explosion of new movements and new communities within the Catholic Church is a fruit of the rediscovery of the 'charismatic' in the Church. 'It is from this providential rediscovery of the Church's charismatic dimension that before and after the Council, there has been a remarkable development of ecclesial movements and new communities.' This is a huge claim concerning the renewal thrust of Vatican II.

In the week before Pentecost 1998, there was a congress in Rome, organized by the Pontifical Council for the Laity, to which leaders of the ecclesial movements and new communities had been invited. The then Cardinal Joseph Ratzinger, now Benedict XVI, gave an important and encouraging address. The distinctive character of the charismatic movement lacking a human founder was implicitly recognized in these invitations.[1] Whereas the new ecclesial movements, begun by visionary founders and foundresses, were all invited movement by movement, many charismatic Catholics were invited under different headings: besides representatives from the international Catholic Charismatic Renewal (CCR), separate invitations were sent to the Rinnovamento nello Spirito Santo in Italy, and to many of the new charismatic communities in the Catholic Church.[2]

The Characteristics of the New Movements

Among the post-Vatican II characteristics of the new movements, we can note:
- their lay character,
- the inclusion of married people and families in movement and community life,
- an emphasis on the Scriptures and on a biblical formation,
- a zeal for evangelization,
- the role of a renewed participatory liturgy in their corporate life,
- an ecumenical dimension,
- dialogue beyond the boundaries of the Catholic Church,
- a love for the poor.[3]

Rather than describing each new movement in the Catholic Church in turn, I will focus on ways in which the best known of these movements embody these characteristics of the post-conciliar Church. For this purpose I will refer to new charismatic communities within CCR as well as to the other new ecclesial movements.

Their Lay Character

The new ecclesial movements and the new communities are overwhelmingly a lay phenomenon. This point was recognized by the Pope when they were placed in the care of the Pontifical Council for the Laity formed after the Council.[4] Many of the founders and foundresses have been lay people, along with the vast majority of their membership.

Among the new movements with lay founders or foundresses are: the Focolari movement; l'Arche; the neo-Catechumenate;[5] the Community of Sant' Egidio; Couples for Christ.[6] Among the charismatic communities with lay founders are the Word of God (Ann Arbor, Michigan, USA); Emmanuel (Brisbane, Australia); Hephzibah Community (Canberra, Australia); Emmanuel (Paris, France); the People of Praise (Notre Dame, Indiana, USA); Alleluia (Augusta, Georgia, USA); the Béatitudes (France); Pain de Vie (France); Comunità di Gesù (Bari, Italy); Light of Jesus Christ Community (Kota Kinabalu, Malaysia); Glory to God Community (Malta), Umkehr zum Herrn (Vienna, Austria).[7] In fact, very few of the new charismatic communities have priest-founders.[8]

It is noteworthy that a group focusing on the conversion and full ecclesial initiation of new believers like the neo-Catechumenate should be founded by a layman, Kiko Arguello.[9] It is more remarkable that forty years later, neo-

Catechumenate, still led by Arguello, is running over thirty missionary seminaries. It is also worth noting that in the new communities teaching is regularly given by lay leaders – not just theological education, as in seminaries and universities, but practical life-oriented teaching of a kind traditionally reserved to ordained ministers.

The lay character of the new movements and communities has produced a new pattern of relationships between clergy and laity. The Foyers de Charité, literally Homes of Love, founded in France in 1936 by a lay woman stigmatic, Marthe Robin (1902–81), aided by Fr Georges Finet (1898–1990), pioneered the first communities with priests and lay people living together: in the Foyers each home is led by a priest but the other residents are lay men and lay women consecrated to the single life. The pattern of close fellowship between lay people and priests also characterized the vision of Pierre Goursat, the founder of Emmanuel Community in Paris, and is found in many new communities in which priest members serve and sometimes live alongside the lay members.

The Inclusion of Married People and Families

As predominantly lay realities, the new ecclesial movements and new communities have included married people and families in their membership (or participants).[10] This represents a significant new development in the history of the Church, that has perhaps not been sufficiently noted. Prior to the Council, there had been a few attempts by lay people to form committed communities, but these had remained very small, and did not usually survive beyond the first generation. It is especially within CR that patterns of community living including lay people and families have developed and flourished. In the USA and Australia, these have mostly taken the form of families owning or renting their own homes, but clustering in the same neighbourhood or suburb so as to facilitate a corporate life-style. In continental Europe, the new communities have often taken over old religious houses, within which families can be accommodated, in effect having their own apartments, but sharing in the communal life of the whole house.[11] This pattern is particularly evident in the more monastic of the new communities, such as the Béatitudes and Pain de Vie that both originated in France.

The Primacy of the Scriptures

One of the first movements to give a central place to the Scriptures was the Young Christian Workers (YCW), founded in Belgium by Fr (later Cardinal) Cardijn in the 1920s. As part of their formation, the YCW began every session with reflection on a passage from the Gospels, using a methodology they also applied to study of their living and working situations: the method of See, Judge and Act.

The Focolari were one of the first movements to give a prominent place to the Gospels. Founded by a young woman, Chiara Lubich (1920–), in Trento, northern Italy, during the darkest years of World War II, the young women drawn to Chiara meditated on the words of Jesus in the Gospel during meetings in air-raid shelters. Some verses were deeply impressed on their hearts, that subsequently shaped the calling of the Focolari movement. Among these were: 'A new commandment I give to you, that you love one another, even as I have loved you, that you also love one another.' (John 13:34) and '[I pray] that they all may be one; even as thou, Father, art in me, and I in thee, that they also may be in us, so that the world may believe that thou has sent me.' (John 17:21). Living in the love of Jesus is central for the Focolari, which requires constant meditation on the person of Jesus as presented in the Gospels.

The Community of Sant' Egidio, founded in Rome during the student disturbances of 1968, also found new life in the Scriptures, which then became a central element in their community life.[12] 'Living and listening to the Word of God as the most important thing in one's own life means accepting that one should follow Jesus, rather than oneself.'[13]

The Proclamation of the Gospel

Several movements not only based their shared life on the Scriptures, but also heard the call to make proclamation of the Gospel message in evangelization central in their apostolate.

One of the first movements to understand the need for a new evangelization through the proclamation of the basic Gospel message was the Cursillo, founded by a Spanish bishop, Mgr Juan Hervas in 1949. Cursillo spread beyond Spain in 1953, and reached the USA in 1962. The Cursillo (literally, little course) was a three-day residential meeting presenting the basic Christian message in a way that enabled the participants to experience a conversion of heart, but in the context of a group undergoing the same experience. The first day was given over to the basic Christian message (and thus had a strong Scriptural content); the second to the faith-response of conversion; and the third to faith lived out in the world. The Cursillo thus anticipated the Christocentric conversion-oriented renewal emphases of the post-conciliar ecclesial movements.

The movement Comunione e Liberazione (CL) traces its origins back to 1954, and a priest's apostolate among high school students in Milan.[14] A young professor of religion at a Milanese high school, Fr Luigi Giussani, later Monsignor (1922–2005), saw the weaknesses of normal Catholic acculturation of the youth, and realized that it was not sufficient just to impart moral principles and church loyalty without imparting a Christian ethos. So he formed student groups in which young people would encounter Jesus, not just in an individual experience but in the company of Jesus, that is in the living church community. In fact, on the basis of this experience, Fr Giussani sought to develop a philosophy of the religious sense that is present throughout humanity and of its transformation through Christ.[15] This philosophy has its own distinctiveness, but it has much in common with the philosophy of John Paul II. From this reflection came the distinctive CL emphasis on both evangelization and inculturation. This Christ-centredness required a greater attention to the Scriptures, especially the Gospels.

Another leader to grasp the essential place of proclamation of the Word of God in eliciting faith was the Polish priest, Fr Franciszek Blachnicki (1921–87), the founder of the Oasis movement that was later re-named Light-Life. In post-war Communist Poland, church movements were banned. The Oasis movement developed as a ministry of Fr Blachnicki to altar servers, for whom he organized occasional retreats. These had such an impact on the boys, that as they grew through adolescence they wanted to continue in this formation from Fr Blachnicki. Fr Blachnicki understood that he had to preach the Word of God to these Polish youth. So it was totally in line with his convictions that he welcomed the Second Vatican Council with great enthusiasm. Unusually in Catholic Poland, Fr Blachnicki instinctively grasped the importance of ecumenism, and perhaps uniquely at that time understood that authentic ecumenism has to lead to ecumenical evangelization. He saw that Evangelical

Protestants knew how to win others to Christ, and he wanted the young Catholics in Oasis to have this ability. So he approached Campus Crusade for Christ (CCC) and asked them to help train his young people in evangelism. The CCC leaders agreed to Fr Blachnicki's condition that they do nothing to alienate these young Catholics from their Catholic faith. In 1982, after Fr Blachnicki had welcomed the CCR, he authorized a period of collaboration with another Protestant para-church agency, Youth With A Mission, which had a charismatic component, not welcomed at that time in CCC.

In general, the new charismatic communities have been among the most evangelistic. Emmanuel Community in Paris was the pioneer of new and creative forms of street evangelism in the big city. Emmanuel's experience and impact in this area was a major factor in the invitation of four cardinal archbishops to help organize city missions in four major European capitals between 2003 and 2006.[16] In 1984, Emmanuel had founded l'Ecole Internationale d'Evangélisation, now based at Paray-le-Monial. Also in 1984, another French movement, Jeunesse-Lumière (Youth-Light), founded by Fr Daniel-Ange, launched its own School of Prayer and Evangelization. These initiatives were soon followed by the Glory to God Community from Malta, who launched the International Catholic Programme for Evangelization (ICPE), now having centres in several nations. Soon after, Fr Tom Forrest CSSR, a major leader in

CCR, as part of the Decade of Evangelization, helped to pioneer many new Schools for Evangelization.

A Renewed Liturgy

In the new ecclesial movements, the vernacular liturgy introduced at Vatican II has come into its own. The neo-Catechumenate has a strongly liturgical and baptismal character. At some meetings they just celebrate liturgies of the Word, and at others the Word is followed by the liturgy of the Eucharist. The celebration of the former heightens the celebration of the latter. The Community of Sant' Egidio formed around daily liturgies, initially in the Church of Sant' Egidio in Rome and later in the larger basilica of Santa Maria in Trastevere. Each evening there is sung vespers, before an icon of the Lord, followed by small groups meeting all around the basilica. The exposition of the Scriptures plays a central role in the community's liturgies, together with a clear application to daily life.

In the movements with residential communities, the celebration of the daily liturgy is central to their community life, as in most traditional religious communities, but there is often a more regular exposition of the Scriptures, a greater creativity in music, more spontaneous intercession, and a greater scope for sensitive adaptation. Liturgies within CCR often give scope for exercise of various charisms within the overall structure of the Eucharist and of the daily office.

Ecumenically Open

The first new movement to develop an ecumenical dimension appears to have been Focolari. Being born amidst the ravages of war, the Focolarini had a strong desire to promote peace and unity through love and reconciliation. In their first years, the focus was on reconciliation between the nations that had been at war, but with the advent of Pope John XXIII, this was extended to cover reconciliation between divided Christian churches and communions. As a result, the Focolari movement opened itself to membership of Christians from other communions, especially Lutherans, Anglicans and Orthodox. The Focolari has thus become the most ecumenical of all the new ecclesial movements. The Focolari had from the start focused on the Trinity as the supreme model for love in total communion, and they readily understood that the renewal of the Church calls for an ecclesial communion of love modelled on and sharing in the communion of Father, Son and Holy Spirit. As Catholic ecclesiology has increasingly centred on the concept of communion, the Focolari have understood that this theology has to be sustained by a spirituality of Church lived as communion in love.

The Cursillo has also developed with an ecumenical dimension. In their case, this was not the result of Cursillo having a particular interest in ecumenism, but because other

Christians, especially Anglicans, came to appreciate the biblical basis and ecclesial sense of the Cursillo, and began to use the Cursillo materials and methods.

Another community with an ecumenical dimension is L'Arche, the community incorporating handicapped people on the same level as the 'non-handicapped'. In the vision of Jean Vanier, the founder of L'Arche, the community would have a Christian inspiration, and at the centre would be a chapel with reservation of the Blessed Sacrament, but they would welcome participants from other churches and faiths, whether among the handicapped or the 'non-handicapped'. Thus, while an ecumenical dimension was not directly intended, this element is found among its fruits.

Several of the new charismatic communities have an ecumenical membership. This is particularly true of the People of Praise (South Bend, Indiana) and Alleluia Community (Augusta, Georgia) in the United States, of the People of God Community (Beirut, Lebanon) and of Umkehr zum Herrn (Vienna, Austria). The Chemin Neuf community, founded in France, describes itself as 'a Catholic community with an ecumenical calling'.

Dialogue

Obviously the changes introduced at Vatican II have impacted all the new ecclesial movements. Several are deeply involved in dialogical approaches to those outside the

Catholic communion, as indicated above under 'Ecumenically Open'. But probably the two movements that have done most to enter into dialogue with people of all faiths are the Focolari and the Community of Sant' Egidio.

In June 2003, Chiara Lubich, the foundress of the Focolari movement, came to London for several meetings. One included leaders from the Muslim and Sikh communities. The Focolari are people of dialogue, listening first to the others before they speak. They do not hide their own convictions, but they want first to know the culture, the language and the faith of the other community. This prepares the ground for them to share their own convictions. It is what they call 'Proclamation with respect'.

The dialogue of Sant' Egidio with those of other faiths and of none arose from their friendship with the poor. They came to see that 'war is the mother of poverty'. As a result, 'love for poor people, in many situations, became work for peace'[17]. So Sant' Egidio leaders played a major role in the peace agreement, reached in Mozambique in 1992 between the government and the rebel Renamo movement. They have played important mediating roles in other conflicts, e.g. in Guatemala and in Algeria. Where working for peace is not yet possible, the Community seeks to bring humanitarian aid to the civilian populations who suffer most from war. In the same sphere of work, the Pope has asked Sant' Egidio to host the inter-faith dialogues that have taken place each year since the Assisi meeting of 1987.

Solidarity with the Poor

Several of the new ecclesial movements and communities are deeply involved with the poor. As has just been mentioned, L'Arche, the community of Jean Vanier, has handicapped people as full participants in their life. The Community of Sant' Egidio has 'solidarity with the poor' as one of its stated goals. The students of 1968 who began gathering around the Word of God, felt the gospel could not be lived far from poor people: poor people as friends and the Gospel as the Good News for poor people. As a result, the first service of the community was called the 'People's School' because it was not simply providing extra tutoring for drop-out children of the slums of Rome, but it was the beginning of a friendship between the rich and the poor. Since then, the people's schools multiplied, in Rome and in all the other cities where the community lives.[18]

Among the charismatic communities, the Pain de Vie community in France has had a special love and care for the poor. Founded in 1975 by a young couple, Pascal and Marie-Annick Pingault, who had been converted out of an anarchist life-style, the Pain de Vie community were struck by the words of Jesus in Luke 4 about proclaiming the Good News to the poor. The life of Pain de Vie is centred around eucharistic adoration and the welcome of the poor and needy, who have been referred to them. They see the second flowing from the first.[19] The poor whom they welcome share fully in the community's life. 'These people must manifest a desire to share our life in truth. We only have Christ to offer them. If not, we try to put them in touch with other non-confessional welcoming agencies.'[20] 'We ensure the evangelization of the poor in fully taking on their material and spiritual distress, by offering them not only hospitality or a welcoming framework and helps external to the community but by inviting them to live with us.'[21] They now have several houses in five other European nations, in Africa, North and South America.[22]

Pentecost 2006

Benedict XVI has long been a supporter of the new ecclesial movements, sensing their importance for the renewal of the whole Church. As an expression of this appreciation, the new Pope repeated the 1998 invitation of his predecessor for the new movements and communities in the Catholic Church to celebrate the feast of Pentecost 2006 with him in Rome. In his message of encouragement, Benedict XVI spoke of 'the true freedom of the children of God' that comes from the Holy Spirit: 'The ecclesial movements want to be, and must be, schools of freedom, of this true freedom.' Life, freedom and unity go together, the Pope said, because as the Spirit generates new gifts, we see how different are the groups that he creates. In him, 'multiplicity and unity go together. He blows where He will. He does so unexpectedly, in unexpected places and in previously unimagined forms. ...

Multiformity and unity are inseparable.' In the view of Benedict XVI, it is the task of the pastors to 'ensure that the Spirit is not extinguished', and the task of the new movements 'to carry your gifts to the entire community.'

Notes

[1] While for the Vatican's pastoral oversight, CCR is considered one of the new ecclesial movements, it differs significantly from the other ecclesial movements, as it did not have a human founder. CCR arose spontaneously out of the action of the Holy Spirit upon a number of Catholics, which led to their forming prayer groups and communities. Whereas the other new movements arose from the vision and commitment of their founders, the leadership of CCR arose out of an unexpected current of grace, for which the meaning had then to be sought out. While CCR in its origins was an unplanned and spontaneous current, subsequently, new charismatic communities were founded, parallel to the other new movements, with founders with a call and a vision into which they drew others.

[2] Of the delegates, who participated in this congress, at least 54 out of 224 came from the CCR.

[3] The last three characteristics only characterize a minority of the new movements and communities.

[4] While the clergy and religious come under the Roman Congregations, which are instruments of government, the laity come under a Pontifical Council, which is an advisory body.

[5] In fact, the neo-Catechumenate do not regard themselves as a 'movement' and only accepted participation in the 1998 Congress as 'observers'. However, from a sociological and existential point of view, they are similar to the new ecclesial movements, and are so treated in this chapter.

[6] Earlier, the Legion of Mary was founded by an Irish layman, Frank Duff, but its ethos belongs rather to the pre-Vatican Two 'lay apostolate'.

[7] In a few of these communities, married lay founders have subsequently been ordained as deacons.

[8] Among those with priest-founders are Chemin Neuf (Lyon, France); Puits de Jacob (Strasbourg, France); Maranatha (Brussels, Belgium), Emanuel (Rio de Janiero, Brazil).

[9] The Neo-Catechumenate was founded in Madrid in 1964. Arguello was joined in the leadership at an early date by a religious, Sr Carmen Hernandez.

[10] Some new movements like Comunione e Liberazione and the Community of Sant' Egidio have deliberately avoided formal patterns of membership.

[11] The Umkehr zum Herrn Community in Vienna, Austria, has also followed the suburban pattern.

[12] Sant'Egidio now has about 50,000 members worldwide (information from www.santegidio.it).

[13] From the website.

[14] CL today has 48,000 members in 64 nations.

[15] Giussani's thought has three main stages: (1) a study of the human heart and its longing that finds fulfilment only in God; (2) a focus on the Jesus-event in which God answers the longing that he has placed in the human heart; (3) an examination of how those who live later than Christ encounter this event and experience transformation. It is at stage three that for Giussani the Church is indispensable for knowing Christ. On Giussani's thought, see Elisa Buzzi (ed.), *A Generative Thought* (Montreal & Kingston: McGill-Queen's University Press, 2003).

[16] Vienna (2003), Paris (2004), Lisbon (2005) and Brussels

(2006). Since the series began, Budapest (2007) has been added to the list.

[17] Also from the Sant' Egidio website.

[18] This information is from the Community's website.

[19] This combination is expressed in the title of a collection of a book produced by the founders and entitled *Pain de Vie Pain des Pauvres* [Bread of Life Bread of the Poor] (Paris, Fayard, 1988).

[20] Pascal Pingault, *Les Communautés Nouvelles* (Paris: Fayard, 1989), p. 185.

[21] Ibid., p. 185.

[22] One of Pascal Pingault's books is translated into English, entitled *Sharing Poverty*.

Church *Forward*

CHAPTER THIRTEEN
The New Synthesis of John Paul II

One of the most important legacies of John Paul II to the Catholic Church is his bringing together into one coherent vision the whole of Catholic magisterial teaching. At the heart of this synthesis is his teaching on the dignity of the human person and on the incarnate Christ as embodying God's plan for humanity.

It is possible that the greatest contribution of John Paul II to the renewal of the Church has been his new synthesis of Catholic magisterial teaching. The Pope from Poland did not just write a number of influential encyclicals or add a significant dimension in some areas. He brought the full range of Catholic teaching into a coherent whole. Much more than most Popes, John Paul II was the primary author of the documents that bear his name. We can see this from the way in which his teachings as Pope are in full continuity with his earlier teaching as philosopher and as bishop in Poland. The key concepts in the Polish period became key concepts in his papacy.

The Weaknesses Remedied

To understand this remarkable achievement of John Paul II, it is helpful to identify the structural weaknesses in Catholic teaching as it was handed down at least from the eighteenth century until the time of the Second Vatican Council. It was marked by major dichotomies. There was a split between dogmatic theology and moral theology; a split between moral theology and spiritual (ascetical) theology; and therefore also a split between dogmatic theology and spiritual theology. All three subjects had become separate disciplines, with dogma and moral theology as major subjects (in pre-Vatican II days taught only to clerical students and to priests), and ascetical theology as a minor course (if it was taught at all in the seminaries) or a specialized subject for spiritually high-flying religious, like Carmelites and Jesuits likely to become confessors and spiritual directors to contemplative nuns. None of these disciplines was directly related to the study of Sacred Scripture. Occasional Bible verses were cited to prove the correctness of Catholic teaching on this or that point, but the decisive arguments came with the citation of St Thomas Aquinas and/or magisterial documents.

In addition, what was called moral theology contained very little theology. A glance at the manuals of moral theology everywhere in use until the time of the Council will illustrate this weakness. Not more than a third of the course taught in seminaries treated basic moral principles, and this third was primarily scholastic philosophy with very little reference to the Judaeo-Christian revelation. Another third perhaps was devoted to the training of priests as confessors (seminaries were mandated by the Council of Trent to remedy the abuse of ignorant priests) by attempting to provide ready-made answers to every imaginable form of individual human deviance. The other third was Canon Law: what has to be done or avoided, because it is required or prohibited in the Church's law. It was to remedy this state of affairs that, in the 1950s, a German Redemptorist, Fr Bernard Häring, wrote a three-volume work entitled *The Law of Christ* in an attempt to produce a genuinely Christian and Catholic moral theology, grounded in the Scriptures and centred on the person and teaching of Christ.

Somewhat similarly to moral theology, Catholic social teaching as it had been formulated since the time of Leo XIII was heavily dependent on natural law and a scholastic ethic, and was not really integrated with any of the theological disciplines. However, its condition was less disastrous than that of moral theology, because it represented a genuinely new interaction of the Church with society, first with the world of capital and labour, and later with the world of developing nations.

The Pope's Preparation

In retrospect, it is not hard to see how Karol Wojtyla was prepared from his youngest years for the task that was to be his as Pope. As a young priest he completed two doctorates, one in theology and one in philosophy. His first doctoral thesis was on the understanding of faith in St John of the Cross. This raised the issue of the relationship between theology and spirituality. His subsequent doctoral studies in philosophy centred on the understanding of the human person. This combination grounded the possibility of Fr Wojtyla's later achievement as Pope: that the following of Jesus Christ could be underpinned by an adequate philosophy of the human person and that this personalist philosophy could be integrated with his Christological faith.

The formative years of Fr Karol Wojtyla were years of great suffering for his people and for his land. First, there was the tyranny and brutality of Nazi occupation, and then, virtually without respite, the imposition of the alien ideology of atheist Communism. As Fr Wojtyla was led to reflect on the human person, he was in no danger of an idealistic theorizing out of touch with the harsh reality that surrounded him. An adequate philosophy of the human person had to allow for the evil and the suffering that he had known and was still witnessing. A constant element in the oppression experienced under both Nazism and Communism was the suppression of the freedom of the person and the denial of human responsibility. The devastating effects of these tyrannies upon society and culture meant that there could be no flight into an individualist or merely existentialist philosophy.

The struggle with Communism marked Fr Wojtyla more even than the struggle against Nazism. It is true that the Nazi oppression gave him first-hand evidence of the radical evil of anti-Semitism and deepened his love for the Jewish people, but the oppression of Communism lasted much longer, and was accompanied by wholesale ideological indoctrination in a way that the Nazis had never attempted for subjugated peoples. This process necessitated an intellectual combat with Marxist atheism. Because Marxism was above all a system emphasizing collectivity and materialism, a Christian refutation had to do justice to the social dimension of human existence and to the place of the body in human life. Here again we find key elements in John Paul's synthesis being prepared many years in advance: a Christian vision of human society and a theology of the body.

Gaudium et Spes

The Second Vatican Council was a formative experience for the young Polish bishop, introducing him to new areas of Catholic thinking, especially of liturgy and ecumenism. But Mgr Wojtyla also made a contribution. He was too young to become a major figure of the Council, but he made a mark in the Pastoral Constitution *Gaudium et spes* on the Church in the Modern World. As a member of the joint commission that drafted *Gaudium et spes,* he contributed to the philosophy of the human person expressed in this document, and especially to the sections on atheism (paras. 19-21).

In *Gaudium et spes* we see for the first time in a magisterial document some of the elements that will be developed by John Paul II. First, there is the concern to ground the Catholic understanding of humanity and the world in a Christocentric theological vision. Thus each of the four chapters in Part I on 'The Church and Man's Vocation' ends by relating its teaching to the person of Christ. Chapter 1 on 'The Dignity of the Human Person' ends with 'Christ the New Man' (para. 22); Chapter 2 on 'The Community of Mankind' with 'The Word Made Flesh and Human Solidarity' (para. 32); Chapter 3 on 'Man's Activity in the Universe' with 'Human Activity: Its Fulfilment in the Paschal Mystery' (paras. 38-39); and Chapter 4 on the 'Role of the Church in the Modern World' with 'Christ: Alpha and Omega' (para. 45). We can see here how this relating of a theology of earthly realities to Christology utilizes images of Christ from the New Testament (Word of God, New Adam, Alpha and Omega) that had been neglected in classical Christology. Second, the document begins with the dignity of the human person, a central theme in the philosophy of Mgr Wojtyla. Sections deal with the dignity of human conscience, and the excellence of freedom, again central themes in his personalist philosophy.

The First Encyclical

In spring 1979, John Paul II issued his first encyclical, *Redemptor hominis*, that was really a vision statement for his pontificate. This encyclical binds together the centrality of Jesus Christ and the dignity of the human person. The Pope makes this connection in the first paragraph: 'Through the Incarnation God gave human life the dimension that he intended man to have from his first beginning' (RH, para. 1). He makes absolutely clear that Jesus Christ is the centre. He draws on a wide range of New Testament texts:

> we must constantly aim at him "who is the head", "through whom are all things and through whom we exist", who is both "the way, and the truth" and "the resurrection and the life", seeing whom we see the Father, and who had to go away from us that is, by his death on the Cross and then by his Ascension into heaven in order that the Counsellor should come to us and should keep coming to us as the Spirit of truth. In him are "all the treasures of wisdom and knowledge", and the Church is his Body (RH, para. 7).

John Paul II goes on to spell out more clearly the relationship between Jesus Christ, God made man, and the dignity of every human person: 'Christ, the Redeemer of the world, is the one who penetrated in a unique unrepeatable way into the mystery of man and entered his "heart"' (RH, para. 8). He then cites his favourite passage from *Gaudium et spes*: 'Christ the new Adam, in the very revelation of the mystery of the Father and of his love, *fully reveals man to himself* and brings to light his most high calling' (RH, para. 8). Later he explicitly links this Christology with the teaching of the Council on Religious Liberty: 'The *Declaration on Religious Freedom* shows us convincingly that, when Christ, and after him his Apostles, proclaimed the truth that comes not from men but from God..., they preserved...a deep esteem for man, for his intellect, his will, his conscience and his freedom' (RH, para. 12).[1]

Thus, in a creatively new way in magisterial teaching, John Paul II combines in his understanding of the incarnation both dogmatic theology and the science of the human person; God and the human are united in Jesus Christ. The science of God and the science of the human are united in this Christology. This combination is central for the renewal of the human person and of human society. From this more theoretical beginning, the Pope goes on to address many of the major issues facing humankind towards the end of the twentieth century. The deepest question is this: 'Does this progress, which has man for its author and promoter, make human life on earth "more human" in every aspect of that life? Does it make it more "worthy of man"?... This question must be put by Christians, precisely because Jesus Christ has made them so universally sensitive about the problem of man' (RH, para. 15). What does 'more human' mean? A few lines further, we find an answer: 'more mature spiritually, more aware of the dignity of his humanity, more responsible, more open to others, especially the neediest and the weakest, and readier to give and to aid all' (RH, para. 15).

Because John Paul II takes human experience seriously, his teaching contains much reflection on new events and contemporary developments. Paul VI had been the first Pope to adopt such a methodology,[2] and John Paul II carries it further. Such reflection especially characterizes *Centesimus annus* (1991), the encyclical in which the Pope reflects on the historic events of 1989 with the fall of the Berlin Wall and the collapse of Communism in Eastern Europe. In 1998, he devoted an entire encyclical, *Fides et ratio,* to the bringing together of faith and reason: here characteristically the first chapter begins with 'Jesus, revealer of the Father', immediately followed by 'Reason before the mystery'. Of particular interest for the renewal of the Church, for both Christian theology and the philosophy of Christians, are the comments of the Holy Father on the importance of the Bible for reflection on all aspects of the human condition: 'In Sacred Scripture are found elements, both implicit and explicit, which allow a vision of the human being and the world which has exceptional philosophical density' (FR, para. 80).

A More Biblical Teaching

As we can already sense from *Redemptor hominis,* the teaching of John Paul II comes from a profound meditation on Sacred Scripture. This has led to papal teaching becoming much more biblical. We can take as one example papal teaching on the Holy Spirit. Since encyclical letters became a major teaching tool of the Popes, there have been two encyclicals on the Holy Spirit: *Divinum illud munus* of Leo XIII (1897) and *Dominum et vivificantem* of John Paul II (1986). The former is only a quarter of the length of the latter. But the encyclical of John Paul II reflects both his own rooting in the Scriptures and a century of renewal of Catholic biblical scholarship. The letter of Leo XIII cites the Scriptures, and particularly the New Testament, much more frequently than most encyclicals before Pius XII. But the structure of his teaching comes from a traditional Catholic framework, which then cites Scripture verses to support and clarify the teaching. But John Paul II's encyclical on the Holy Spirit is much more thoroughly biblical, both in its structure and in its teaching. I will simply cite some chapter headings that treat of biblical themes not mentioned or only given one sentence by Leo XIII:

I.4   The Messiah, anointed by the Holy Spirit
5.   Jesus of Nazareth, 'exalted' in the Holy Spirit
6.   The Risen Christ says, 'Receive the Holy Spirit'
II.1   Sin, righteousness and judgment
5.   The blood that purifies the conscience
6.   The sin against the Holy Spirit
III.3 The Holy Spirit in man's inner conflict: 'For the desires of the flesh are against the Spirit, and the desires of the Spirit are against the flesh'
4.   The Holy Spirit strengthens the 'inner man'
6.   The Spirit and the Bride say: 'Come!'

We can see here the impact of biblical reflection on the Holy Spirit in the life of Jesus himself, as well as an integration of the dogmatic relationship of Jesus to the Holy Spirit and the moral teaching concerning the inner conflict in the life of the Christian. Another more biblical aspect in John Paul II's teaching is its heightened Trinitarian character. In fact, the encyclical *Dominum et vivificantem* on the Holy Spirit completed a Trinitarian trilogy, following his first encyclical on Christ the Redeemer (*Redemptor hominis*) and then one on the Father, *Dives in misericordia* (1980).

Two other encyclicals of John Paul II illustrate very clearly the biblical foundation and the integration of the dogmatic and the moral: *Veritatis splendor* (1993), the encyclical on moral teaching, and *Evangelium vitae* (1995), treating the value and inviolability of human life. Both begin in an unprecedented way with a long biblical meditation. The moral teaching begins with a meditation on the story of the rich young man (Matt. 19:16-26)[3] and that on human life with a meditation on the story of Cain and Abel (Gen. 4:2-16).[4] The Pope enters deeply into both these narratives to draw forth the basic elements in his teaching.

The Teaching on Mary

It is well known that Pope John Paul II had a great love for Mary, the Mother of the Lord. What is less well known is the way his teaching on Mary carried further the Council's integration of Mariology into the mystery of the Church and its desire for a biblically-based theology. We see this especially in his encyclical *Redemptoris mater* (1987), in which the first part 'Mary in the Mystery of Christ' examines the biblical data concerning Mary and her relationship to the person and mission of her Son. The Pope particularly emphasized the faith of Mary, comparing the faith of Mary to the faith of Abraham: 'In the salvific economy of God's revelation, Abraham's faith constitutes the beginning of the Old Covenant; Mary's faith at the Annunciation inaugurates the New Covenant' (RM, para. 14). Later he took up this point again: 'In the expression "Blessed is she who believed," we can therefore rightly find a kind of "key" which unlocks for us the innermost reality of Mary, whom the angel hailed as "full of grace"' (RM, para. 19).

Redemptoris mater is fully in continuity with Chapter 8 of *Lumen gentium* on Our Lady. The encyclical shows clearly how the inclusion of Mary in the teaching of the Church was in no way a demotion of Marian devotion, but a recentring on the one mystery of Christ. Part II deals with 'The Mother of God at the Centre of the Pilgrim Church'. The Holy Father's strong sense of history and his place in leadership at the end of the second millennium shine through in this section. Mary is the one 'who "precedes" us all at the head of the long line of witnesses of faith in the one Lord' (RM, para. 30).[5] He takes up *Lumen gentium's* focus on the motherhood of Mary, and develops it into Part III on 'Maternal Mediation'. Everything concerning Mary's role flows from her unique motherhood, first of Jesus and then of his disciples.

Another facet of John Paul II's contribution to a synthesis of Catholic teaching is implicit in his surprising decision to add five luminous mysteries to the Rosary. Catholic piety has long paid particular attention to the nativity and to the passion of Christ, a twin focus that was symbolized in the Rosary, where one jumped straight from the joyful childhood to the sorrowful passion. With the addition of five luminous mysteries,[6] the Holy Father brought the life and ministry of the adult Christ into the heart of Catholic meditation upon the incarnate Son of God.

Social Teaching

John Paul II wrote three encyclical letters explicitly devoted to Catholic social teaching: *Laborem exercens* (1981), *Sollicitudo rei socialis* (1987) and *Centesimus annus* (1991). Near the end of his pontificate, he authorized the publication of the first *Compendium of Catholic Social Teaching* (2004).

The 1987 and 1991 encyclicals did not begin from a personalist theological position because they were issued on the anniversaries of major social encyclicals and so started from an assessment of the contribution of previous Popes.[7] However, John Paul II's characteristic integration of the human and the theological can be seen from later chapters in *Sollicitudo rei socialis*, in which Chapter IV deals with 'Authentic Human Development' and Chapter V with 'A Theological Reading of Modern Problems'. In Chapter VI of *Centesimus annus*, entitled 'Man is the Way of the Church', the Pope outlined again his understanding of the integration of divine revelation and human science: 'Christian anthropology therefore is really a chapter of theology, and for this reason, the Church's social doctrine, by its concern for man and by its interest in him and in the way he conducts himself in the world, "belongs to the field... of theology and particularly of moral theology"' (CA, para. 55).

A Theology of Martyrdom

The great achievement of Pope John Paul II in producing a body of coherent Catholic teaching that brings together all aspects of human existence and life in the Church can also be illustrated by one of his most original contributions: the teaching on martyrdom. Not only have there been more Christian martyrs in the twentieth century than in all previous Christian centuries combined, but in Poland John Paul II lived for many years in a Church that was experiencing martyrdom. So it is not surprising that in his reflection on the clash between the Church and brutal totalitarian regimes he should consider the meaning of Christian martyrdom.

John Paul II first developed his theology of martyrdom in his encyclical on moral teaching. Martyrdom shows forth in 'all its brilliance' the relationship between faith and morality (VS, para. 90). When someone is willing to die rather than contravene the law of God, there is the highest form of witness to the dignity of the human person and the inviolability of conscience (see VS, para. 92). The theology of martyrdom was further developed in the encyclical on ecumenism, *Ut unum sint* (1995). The Pope recognized that all Christian communions have had martyrs for their faith in Christ: 'Despite the tragedy of our divisions, these brothers and sisters have preserved an attachment to Christ and to the

Father so radical and absolute as to lead even to the shedding of blood' (UUS, para. 83).

'In a theocentric [God-centred] vision, we Christians already have a common Martyrology' (UUS, para. 84). This recognition led in the Jubilee Year 2000 to the first-ever common celebration in Rome of martyrs from many different Christian communions. While the relationship between the separated Churches is at present one of 'an imperfect but real communion', the Pope says that with the martyrs who die for Christ 'this communion is already perfect in what we all consider the highest point of the life of grace, *martyria* unto death' (UUS, para. 84). Honouring each other's martyrs is another way of proclaiming the absolute transcendence and centrality of Jesus Christ and his death on the cross.

Gazing Upon the Face of Christ

There is another aspect of the papacy of John Paul II that was connected to his provision of a coherent corpus of Catholic teaching. He is the first Pope who personally described the journey on which he had been leading the Catholic Church. We find such an account in Part I of the Apostolic Letter *Mane nobiscum domine* (2004).[8] The Pope outlined a sequence of events beginning with the preparation for the Great Jubilee of the year 2000, which was focused on the incarnation in a Trinitarian pattern. This focus on Christ was taking up the themes of his first encyclical *Redemptor hominis* (1979), that 'In the Incarnate Word, both the mystery of God and the mystery of man are revealed' (MND, para. 6). At the end of the Jubilee year, the Pope followed with an Apostolic Letter, *Novo millennio ineunte* (2001), saying that the meeting with Christ must lead to our gazing upon his face. 'Our witness would be hopelessly inadequate if we ourselves had not first contemplated his face' (NMI, para. 16). Then, with the Apostolic Letter *Rosarium virginis mariae* (2002), he took up this same theme presenting the five new luminous mysteries of the Rosary as 'a kind of pedagogy of love, aimed at evoking within our hearts the same love that Mary bore for her Son' (MND, para. 9). Lastly, the Year of the Eucharist continued in the same line, centred on Christ and gazing upon his face. In some ways, *Mane nobiscum domine* summarized the vision of John Paul II: the self-giving of Jesus Christ, the only Son of the Father, through the Holy Spirit, that is embodied in the Eucharist. 'The Eucharist is light above all because at every Mass the liturgy of the Word of God precedes the liturgy of the Eucharist in the unity of the two "tables", the table of the Word and the table of the Bread' (MND, para. 12). The Eucharist that is the summit of the Church's worship both nourishes her own life of communion (Part III) and serves as the principle and plan of her mission (Part IV).

Notes

[1] This paragraph continues: 'Thus the human person's dignity itself becomes part of the content of that proclamation, being included not necessarily in words but by an attitude towards it. This attitude seems to fit the special needs of our times' (RH, para. 12).

[2] In the encyclical *Populorum progressio* (1967).

[3] VS, paras. 6-22.

[4] EV, paras. 7-28.

[5] This citation comes from a section on 'The Church's journey and the unity of all Christians'.

[6] The five new mysteries of the Rosary are: (1) the baptism of the Lord; (2) the marriage feast at Cana; (3) the preaching of the Kingdom; (4) the transfiguration on Mount Tabor; and (5) the institution of the Eucharist.

[7] *Sollicitudo rei socialis* commemorates the twentieth anniversary of Paul VI's encyclical *Populorum progressio* (1967) and *Centesimus annus* the centenary of Leo XIII's pioneering encyclical *Rerum novarum* (1891).

[8] See paras. 6-10.

CHAPTER FOURTEEN
A New Ecumenism?

Benedict XVI is making Christian unity a central issue in his pontificate. In his encyclical Ut unum sint John Paul II called for a new appreciation of the 'spiritual ecumenism' urged at the Council. In this new phase of the ecumenical movement, the role of the Holy Spirit will be central. Two new developments are of particular significance: the Catholic repentance for the sins of the past, urged by John Paul II, and the new openings between Catholics and Evangelicals.

The contribution of John Paul II to a renewed Catholic Church will take time to evaluate, though in the last chapter I have given reasons why the coherence of his overall teaching as Pope is of major significance for the Church. But even as I write this, I am aware of a major contrast. On the one hand, Pope John Paul's synthesis is really a European achievement. Further, his project for the 'new evangelization', or the re-evangelization of once Christian societies, has arisen particularly from the critical situation in much of Europe today. On the other hand, the astonishing growth of the Church is above all in Africa. There are many signs that the centre of gravity of the Christian world is moving south, and this is all the more evident when one takes into account the spread of Pentecostal and charismatic forms of Christian faith, not only in Africa, but also in Asia and Latin America.

I began this book with an overview of the dramatic changes within Catholic Christianity during the twentieth century. Then I looked at the major Catholic event of the twentieth century, the Second Vatican Council, from the perspective of the renewal of the Church, followed by significant developments for renewal since the Council. But this shift of Christianity's centre of gravity to the south may lead us to assess the twentieth-century developments somewhat differently.

It is in the continents of Africa, Asia and Latin America that the Church's voice in favour of the dignity of the human person and against all forms of oppression has been the strongest. Witness, for example, the strong voice for the poor of Archbishop Oscar Romero of San Salvador, shot at the altar for his opposition to injustice; and the courageous stance over many years of the former bishop in Dili, East Timor, Mgr Carlos Ximenes Belo. But the indigenization of the Church in these continents has been slow, and the loss of Catholics to new Spirit-type churches has been greatest in Africa and Latin America. The Roman instinct is to retain strong links with the centre in the Vatican and so to minimize local adaptations and regional autonomy. This is a hard issue to evaluate, as for Africa in particular there may be wisdom in this policy given the pressures that the instability of many political regimes places on the Church.

Chapter Fourteen • A New Ecumenism?

The Importance of the Ecumenical Movement

Inevitably perhaps given the methodology of this book, with its reflection on the renewal of the Catholic Church, the focus has been on Catholic developments. It could therefore encourage the false idea that the Catholic Church can be renewed on its own apart from the renewal of other Christian churches and communions. This profound renewal of the Catholic Church taking place in the second half of the twentieth century has been made possible by the Church listening to voices that were previously dismissed. First, a listening to the voices of the Reformation opened the Catholic Church to a new awareness of the role of the Word of God. Second, a listening to the voices of Enlightenment thinkers opened the Catholic Church to a respect for the dignity of every human being and to a recognition of the rights of each person. This listening of the Church has not of course led to an uncritical acceptance of the views of either the Protestants or the philosophers of the Enlightenment, but to an acceptance of a core-idea that is a precondition for any renewal in depth, and its grounding in the biblical revelation.

This listening to the voice of other Christian communities is essential for renewal, because – as Vatican II recognized – the Spirit of God is at work among them. The working of the Holy Spirit in other Christian bodies is not just an anonymous presence like the activity of the Holy Spirit in the world, but an explicit Christ-testifying presence as in the

Catholic Church. Wherever the Spirit of God is bringing the Word of God to life, there is something to be learned from divine revelation, something to be learned about Jesus Christ. This entire revelation is needed for the plan of the Lord to be realized.

We have already seen in Chapter Seven on ecumenism that the Abbé Couturier understood the need for a change from a church-centred view to a Christ-centred position. And that, for Couturier, this was not a change from a corporate to an individualistic position, but from a church institution-centred view to an ecclesially Christocentric position. Instead of starting from our Churches as they are and then comparing doctrines, mentalities, liturgies, etc. we need to start from our Churches before the Lord both in recognizing what they currently are in the Lord's sight and what the Lord calls them to be. Here we can see that John Paul II's call for ecumenical dialogue to have a vertical as well as a horizontal dimension is in fact an application of Couturier's insights to the sphere of dialogue. As the Holy Father said, 'This vertical aspect of dialogue lies in our acknowledgment, jointly and to each other, that we are men and women who have sinned. It is precisely this acknowledgment which creates in brothers and sisters living in Communities not in full communion with one another that interior space where Christ, the source of the Church's unity, can effectively act, with all the power of his Spirit, the Paraclete.' (UUS, para. 35). It is out of this Christ-centred perspective that the question of confessing the sins of the past necessarily arises.

However, as we look at the situation over fifty years after the death of Couturier, we can see that (1) his insights were of major significance; (2) not enough attention was given in his day to the role of the Holy Spirit. Today there is a new consciousness of the role of the Holy Spirit, following the Second Vatican Council, with a new awareness of Eastern Christianity and with the advent of charismatic renewal. What is now becoming increasingly apparent is that what matters in each church heritage is the work of the Holy Spirit. The key question, to be asked first of our own church tradition, is: what is most clearly the work of the Holy Spirit? Then we can ask the same question of other Christian traditions. When we see what is clearly the work of the Holy Spirit (the Protestant love of the Bible, their recognition of the dignity of every Christian believer, the profound hymnody), we should acknowledge this and honour it.

The Foundation for Ecumenical Relations

The Council's Decree on Ecumenism affirmed that 'baptism constitutes the sacramental bond of unity existing among all who through it are reborn'. (UR, para. 22).[1] However, many Christians do not baptize infants and practise what is called 'believers' baptism' of adults (Baptists, Mennonites, most Pentecostals, most new charismatic churches). They do not believe that anyone, whether adult or child, becomes a Christian through baptism. For them, Christians are those who have experienced a clear conversion to Christ. These groups who do not recognize the sacrament of baptism as the foundation for communion among Christians are in fact those who are growing fastest in the world and so currently represent a higher percentage of world Christianity with each passing decade.

Yet it is clearly not the case that it is impossible for Catholics to know communion in Christ with Evangelical Christians. The break-through in Evangelical–Catholic relations came first with the rise of the charismatic movement. For in the charismatic renewal, Christians from widely differing backgrounds discovered that they could worship, pray and serve together because they had experienced the same renewing work of the Holy Spirit. This experience makes clear that a spiritual communion in Christ is possible with any Christians who are willing to turn together in faith to God our Father in the name of Jesus Christ through the working of the Holy Spirit. This development calls for a re-formulation of the statement that sacramental baptism is the ground of all communion between Christians. This does not mean that baptism is not foundational, but that what matters is what the Word of God and the Holy Spirit bring about through the sign of baptism: a sharing in Trinitarian communion. To be a Christian is to enter the fellowship of fellow sons and daughters of the Father, in the

Body of Christ and under His Lordship, and all in the power and through the moving of the Holy Spirit.

Here we can see a development that is totally in line with the new emphasis on the Church as communion. Just as in ecclesiology, we are being pushed back, or drawn deeper, beyond the Church's institutional face, into the fundamental reality of the Church as a sharing in Trinitarian communion, so in ecumenism we are being pushed back beyond the outward sacramental forms to what they inwardly signify and effect, the communion with the Father in Christ through the Spirit.

Two Complementary Thrusts

Here we can glimpse two new openings of recent years that have to be of huge potential significance for the future of ecumenism and thus for the renewal of the Church. Both are as yet in their earliest phases.

The first is repentance for the sins of the past. The Pope has made this call in the framework of 'mainline ecumenism'. While this call was made in the context of the Church's preparation for the Great Jubilee of the year 2000, it is clear from its nature and from the statements just cited on the vertical element in all ecumenical dialogue that this confession of the sins of the past is an essential component for all future ecumenism. But just as the official dialogues have as yet hardly begun to incorporate this essential element, so also this humble acknowledgment of our sinful pasts has not yet found a significant place in wider ecumenical encounters and activities. So this a major agenda item for the future.

The second is the importance of the Catholic–Evangelical encounter. It is the Catholic–Evangelical encounter, particularly as it has been made possible by the charismatic movement, that especially pushes us back to the spiritual foundations of repentance and conversion, and of our relations to Father, Son and Holy Spirit. Here by Evangelical, I am referring to all the evangelical-type groupings that emphasize the authority of the Word of God, the centrality of Jesus Christ and the cross, and the necessity of conversion for each Christian and the primacy of evangelism for the Church.[2] Thus, it is very short-sighted as well as unjust for the historic Churches to dismiss the new Evangelical, Pentecostal and charismatic groupings as "sects" as is still common in many (especially non-English speaking) parts of the world. In an important sense, they represent the Holy Spirit's answer to the stagnation in the ecumenical movement. Where relations with the Evangelicals are taken seriously, there is new life in the quest for unity – and young people are interested in an ecumenism that is rooted in spiritual renewal.

The Catholic Contribution

Of course the Catholic Church has an important contribution to make in the reconstitution of Christian unity. This contribution is deeply bound up with the Catholic sense of the incarnation and of the continuity between the incarnation and the sacraments. The Word comes first, but the Word takes on flesh. This order is foundational for the Church and for ecumenism.

This faith that comes from hearing the Word 'confesses that Jesus Christ has come in the flesh' (1 John 4:2). When people ask Jesus what they are to do, he replies, 'This is the work of God, that you believe in him whom he has sent' (John 6:29). This leads necessarily to belief that the one the Father has sent is 'the bread of life' (John 6:35), whose 'flesh is food indeed' and whose 'blood is drink indeed' (John 6:55).

The Catholic interaction with the Evangelicals confronts us with our reliance on the institutional and the outward in ways that are substitutes for faith rather than expressions of faith. This interaction sends us back to the Word of God. It puts Christ back at the centre. It calls for reliance on the Holy Spirit. But then making our foundation afresh in Christ, we have to return – and to invite the Evangelicals to accompany us – to the Word made flesh, to the Scriptures enacted in a Spirit-filled and Christocentric liturgy.

It is true that Catholic–Evangelical fellowship by itself lacks the objectivity that sacramental communion brings. The sacraments objectify and make more real in our human experience the spiritual reality – the life of the Spirit–that is first awakened and implanted by the Word of God. The problem that we face in the Catholic Church and in ecumenical relations with the historic Churches is that there is widespread celebration of sacraments and liturgy without the prior conversion that only the Word of God can effect. It is for this reason that the interaction – not just theological dialogue – with the Evangelicals is so essential, for it confronts us with the first place of the Word of God and with the priority of conversion.

Yes, as Catholics we do see a foundational importance for baptism as the sacramental expression that anchors our incorporation into Jesus Christ, and the mystery of his death and resurrection. But our trust cannot be in a rite. Our trust is in the Lord who acts in and through this ritual action, that is a faith-act of the Christian community. We can only discover the proper role of baptism as a foundational sign in Christian initiation, when we first honour the place of the Word of God. Only then does baptism express and effect the repentance that the baptismal immersion or washing signifies. Otherwise appealing to baptism as the foundation is in danger of pointing to an outward reality that is masking an underlying inner emptiness rather than manifesting the deeper life of the Holy Spirit.

Chapter Fourteen • A New Ecumenism?

The Contribution of the New Ecumenism

This urging of the importance of the Catholic–Evangelical encounter is not arguing that this is the only ecumenical relationship that matters. But it is saying that the whole ecumenical movement needs this encounter. The Catholic–Evangelical encounter confronts us with what has to be confronted in order that the whole quest for unity may move forward. Besides the focus on the Word of God and conversion, the Catholic–Evangelical encounter will also face us in a new way with another vital component, namely the place of the Jewish people and their importance for the reconstitution of Christian unity.

At first sight, this may seem strange to some readers, as it is the mainline Churches that have opened themselves up to Jewish – Christian dialogue, and it is the Evangelicals who have continued their evangelistic missions to the Jews, which constitute an obstacle to dialogue. Here we find another impasse: dialogue or conversion? But this is another reason why Catholic–Evangelical dialogue is indispensable. It is among Evangelicals that we can find more Christians who understand that a Jewish presence in the Church is essential, both for Christian unity and for hastening the coming of the Lord. But it is among Catholics today that there is a deeper understanding of the role of history and tradition, and the importance of the historic Jewish community. How to relate dialogue and evangelism is thus a major agenda item for the

Catholic – Evangelical encounter. And one of its fruits will be a clearer understanding of the place of the Jewish communities of believers in Jesus the Messiah and Son of God in the reconstitution of the Church's unity and so for the renewal of the whole body of Christ.

Notes

[1] The 1972 Ecumenical Directory says that baptism is "the foundation of communion among all Christians" (para. 11).

[2] 'Evangelical' here then includes the Pentecostals and the 'new' charismatics. In the usage most commonly found on the European continent, it is largely covered by the term 'free church' (freien Gemeinden, églises libres), but this language would be confusing in the British Isles.

PART III

Church *Forward*

PART III

Church *Forward*

PROLOGUE

In Part II, we have looked at significantly new dimensions of renewal in the Catholic Church in the forty years since the end of the Second Vatican Council. This method has advantages and disadvantages. Among the disadvantages is that less attention is paid to the patterns of renewal in areas of Catholic life directly treated by the Council. Very obviously, this includes the place of Our Lady and the place of the Eucharist in Catholic life. These have been touched on in Part II insofar as the renewal of Marian faith and liturgical life are mentioned in the chapters on the new ecclesial movements and on the synthesis of John Paul II. But the advantages of this method are that the distinctively new developments since the Council tell us something important about the renewal of everything in Catholic life. In this respect the chapter on the distinctive contribution of Pope John Paul II illustrates how his profound rootedness in the Catholic tradition and his creativity of spirit flowed together in bringing new life to the historic faith.

Already in Chapter Fourteen, we began to look towards the future, and to indicate areas in which the Holy Spirit is already leading us beyond the great achievements of the Council. This reflection on the renewal of the Church requires some attention to the questions: How far have we come? What remains to be done? I have chosen to do this by reflecting on the three theological virtues: faith, hope and love, though I am changing their order. Ultimately, if efforts at renewal of the Church are not producing a Church of deeper faith, of more intensive love and of more profound hope, then they are failing. In these last three chapters, I will be looking at signs of growth in these three dimensions of church life. These will provide some indications of how far we have come and some challenges as to how far we still have to go. Of course, nobody can measure with full accuracy the levels of faith, love and hope in the Church. But it is possible to see signs of fruit, and to identify challenges for future growth.

CHAPTER FIFTEEN
Believing the Faith

'These are written that you may believe that Jesus is the Christ, the Son of God, and that believing you may have life in his name' (John 20:31).

In this book I have outlined the development of renewal in the twentieth-century Catholic Church. I have looked at the contribution of the Second Vatican Council to this renewal (Part I) and at major renewal developments since the Council (Part II). Two key principles of the Council, both representing radically new emphases in the Catholic Church, are fundamental to this renewal: first, the preaching and hearing of the Word of God (Chapter Three) and, second, the recognition of the dignity of each human person (Chapter Four). Faith comes by hearing the Word, as Paul says in Romans 10:17, and faith is an essentially free act, a free response of the heart that is open to the Word.

All authentic renewal represents a deepening of faith. Not just faith in the sense of what is believed, but also faith as the stance of the believer. The person who receives the Word does not just believe that the Word is objectively true (that Jesus did die on the cross and that he did rise from the dead), but it is also an entrusting of oneself to the person in whom one believes (we entrust our lives to Jesus who died and rose for us). In this chapter, I will look more carefully at what renewal means in terms of a renewed faith.

Really Believing What We Profess

One way of looking at the renewal of the Church is to say that we are called upon to believe with our whole being that faith which we officially and outwardly profess. Mgr Giussani, the founder of Comunione e Liberazione, like the founders of other renewal movements, wrestled with the problem of people leaving the Church. Giussani was deeply affected by a passage from T. S. Eliot's poem *The Rock*, where Eliot asked: 'Has the Church failed mankind, or has mankind failed the Church?' Giussani then saw the problem was that the Church had abandoned the people before the people were leaving the Church. So he wrote: 'The Church began to abandon humankind, when she forgot who Christ is, when she did not depend any longer on him, and...became ashamed to declare who Christ is.'

That is the question: Do we really believe what we say we believe? Perhaps we believe it as objective truth, but subjectively we do not entrust our lives to the Lord we profess. Let us look at some examples.

Believing in the Word of God. For those who are called to public ministry in the Church: do we truly believe in the Word of God that is proclaimed in our liturgy? When we preach, do we believe that there is a power in the Word of God, because it is the Word of God? Could we write about those to whom we preach in the way that St Paul wrote to the Thessalonians: 'And we also thank God constantly for this, that when you received the word of God which you heard from us, you accepted it not as the word of men but as what it really is, the word of God, which is at work in you believers' (1 Thess. 2:13).

If we truly believe in the Word of God, we will preach homilies that enable people to hear the biblical Word today. If we truly believe in the Word of God, we will not think that the people will be bored unless the preacher introduces a bit of entertainment. If we truly believe in the Word of God, we will prepare for preaching more on our knees than at our desks. For we will be depending on the Holy Spirit who inspired the Scriptures to show what we are to say and how we are to say it. For the Holy Spirit knows the lives and the deep needs of our hearers. This is not a recipe for ignoring biblical studies, for it is when we prepare homilies on our knees that the Holy Spirit draws upon our lifelong study of the Scriptures.

Believing in the Presence of Christ in the Liturgy. Do we believe that the risen Jesus Christ is truly present in all the liturgies of the Church? He is present in the consecrated elements of the Eucharist; he is present in the person of the minister; he is present in his Word; he is present in the whole gathered congregation 'for he has promised that "where two or three are gathered together in my name there am I in the midst of them" (Matt. 18:20).'[1] Do we priests preside at the Eucharist conscious of the mutually enriching ways in which the Lord is present? Do we act as those who surrender ourselves in faith to the priestly ministry of Jesus himself? Do we help the other ministers to understand the dignity and importance of their service? When we receive communion, do we believe in the transforming power of Jesus Christ who feeds us with his own body and blood and forms us together into his one body?

God's Word as Personal Word. Do we believe that God speaks to us today? Or do we just think that God spoke two thousand and more years ago, but has been silent ever since? The Letter to the Hebrews says: 'The word of God is living and active, sharper than any two-edged-sword, piercing to the division of soul and spirit, of joints and marrow, and discerning the thoughts and intentions of the heart'

(4:12). This can only happen when God speaks his Word to us in the present. When we do not believe that God speaks today, we do not expect God to speak and we do not ask him to speak. This leads to spiritual impoverishment 'You do not have, because you do not ask' (Jas 4:2).

Organizing Church Meetings. For all of us who are responsible in any way for church meetings, that seek to advance the work and the mission of the Church: how do we plan the agenda for our meetings? Do we seek the light of the Holy Spirit in forming the agenda? Do we pray for light on God's priorities? Indeed, we should ask if there is an overall vision sought out in prayer for the whole life of a diocese, a parish, a school, a sodality, into which each particular meeting fits.

Then how are such meetings structured? What role is played by worship and prayer? Do we act as though the opening prayer is something to be got through before we get down to the real business? It is here that the truth about our faith-relationships comes out. If we truly believe in the love of God the Father, the grace of our Lord Jesus Christ and the communion of the Holy Spirit (see 2 Cor. 13:13), we will show our trust and dependence on the divine Persons in the way that we plan and conduct our meetings.

Sin and Repentance. The Church believes that sin is an offence against God, and weakens or disrupts our communion with God according to its gravity. The Church believes that confession and repentance are essential elements in reconciliation. But how do we actually handle sinful situations in our parishes, particularly in face-to-face groups like liturgy committees and choirs, RCIA, parish councils, social action bodies, prayer groups, etc.? Do we act as though our work for the Lord will not be affected if we allow simmering quarrels and back-biting to continue? Do we prefer a quiet life without conflict to dealing with sin so that there can be healing and spiritual impact?

Intercession. Do we believe in the power of prayer? When we see the number of people attending Mass decreasing, when our congregations are increasingly elderly, do we believe that steadfast and sustained prayer can affect the situation? Perhaps we do believe this, and so we ask the nearest Carmelite sisters to pray for these needs. But do we believe in the power of our own prayers? Really this means: do we believe in the Holy Spirit who dwells within us? The apostle Paul knew this. He said: 'the Spirit himself intercedes for us with sighs too deep for words' (Rom. 8:26).

Evangelization. We will only evangelize others if we truly believe in the gospel of Jesus Christ. It does not require living faith to have a theological or a religious discussion. But to speak to someone else about Jesus Christ as Saviour and as Lord, not just about Christology, requires a deep trust in the One of whom we speak. For in our hearts we know that our words will only sound convincing if they come out of a genuine faith-commitment. This is why the most explicit evangelization in the Catholic Church is taking place in the new ecclesial movements.

Believing in the Holy Spirit. The common element in all these challenges is the Holy Spirit. The Holy Spirit is the bridge between heaven and earth, and the bridge between the first century and the twenty-first. All forms of not deeply believing in the faith we profess outwardly are forms of unbelief in the Holy Spirit.

It is the Holy Spirit who opens up God's revelation to us. The Holy Spirit reveals to us inwardly the person and the teaching of Christ. Jesus says of the Holy Spirit: 'All that the Father has is mine; therefore I said that he [the Holy Spirit] will take what is mine and declare it to you' (John 16:15). This is at the heart of the work of the Holy Spirit: to reveal the reality of Jesus to the eyes of faith. That is why serious renewal begins with invocation of the Holy Spirit, as Blessed John XXIII well understood.

To be renewed is to act as believers, both personally and corporately, as Christians and as church. Being attentive to the Holy Spirit is not escapism; it is not to turn our backs on the realities of this world. It is to relate what we live, what we celebrate, what we suffer, what we like, what we hate, to the Lord of all. It is to relate this world as it is and ourselves as we are to the Lord of all, who shared our sufferings and the most appalling death; it is to bring all to his love, to his mercy and to his purposes. It is to allow the Lord to sort us out and to sort out our real situations, so that the transforming power of his Spirit can enter into this reality and change it from within. Only thus can we fully enter into the amazing plan of the Father 'to bring all things in heaven and on earth together under one head, even Christ' (Eph. 1:10).

Note

[1] Constitution on the Liturgy, para. 7.

CHAPTER SIXTEEN
Lived in Love

'A new commandment I give to you, that you love one another; even as I have loved you, that you also love one another' (John 13: 34).

It is clear from the New Testament that love has to be a sign of the work of the Holy Spirit in the Church. Love is the first fruit of the Spirit that Paul lists in Galatians (5: 22). In fact, Paul insists, without love faith is not enough. 'And if I have prophetic powers, and understand all mysteries and all knowledge, and if I have all faith, so as to remove mountains, but have not love, I am nothing.' (1 Cor. 13: 2).

Love has then to be a criterion for the authentic renewal of the Church. We might adapt Paul's words in 1 Corinthians 13 and say: 'If we have carried out a thorough-going liturgical reform, if we have made our theology more biblical and expressed it in contemporary language, if we have produced impressive new documents on evangelization and catechesis, if we have dynamic new ecclesial movements and new communities, but we have not love, then we are nothing.

Since this chapter was first written, Pope Benedict XVI has emphasized in his first encyclical *Deus caritas est* that this love has to be expressed corporately as well as individually. 'Love of neighbour, grounded in the love of God, is first and foremost a responsibility for each individual member of the faithful, but it is also a responsibility for the entire ecclesial community at every level: from the local community to the particular Church and to the Church universal in its entirety. As a community, the Church must practise love.' (para. 20).

Models

With almost half a century of ecclesial renewal in the Catholic Church, we should expect to have some models whose lives point to the centrality of love at the heart of the Body of Christ. In ecclesial terms, we can ask, in what ways have efforts for the renewal of the Church truly deepened the real life of Trinitarian communion in the Church? I wish to pick out a few examples, each one of which tells us something about the love that the Lord is pouring into his Church.

Blessed John XXIII (1881–1963). We have already seen that Pope John exhibited that trust in God and in the Holy Spirit that was to be a beacon for the Council and for the renewal of the Church. This trust in the Lord was accompanied by a deep love and respect for all the people whom he met. In 1940, in Istanbul, Archbishop Roncalli, as he then was, heard of the fate of the Jews in Nazi-occupied Europe from a group of Jewish refugees. His heart of love was expressed in a letter he wrote to a nun: 'We are dealing with one of the great mysteries in the history of humanity. Poor children of Israel. Daily I hear their groans around me. They are relatives and fellow-countrymen of Jesus.'

The love of Pope John was manifest in his visit to Rome's Regina Coeli prison at Christmas, 1958. It was expressed in the way he related to the prisoners, whom he treated as equals before God. His love for other Christians was evident to the increasing number of church leaders who came to visit him in the Vatican. His love for all people, of whatever religion or political philosophy, was shown in his welcome to Khrushchev's daughter and son-in-law. His heart for the world and its future was revealed in his last encyclical *Pacem in terris*. People recognize love when they see it, and this was manifest in the world's response to Pope John's death.

Blessed Mother Teresa of Calcutta (1910–97). Mother Teresa models the love of Jesus for the most poor and destitute in the world. As is well known, in the 1940s Mother

Teresa left the order to which she belonged to found a new congregation to care for the destitute and the dying. She had been serving in Calcutta, India, for some twenty years, a city where she saw appalling poverty and human suffering. Mother Teresa knew she was called to identify in love with the most poor and the most abandoned. Her life was above all a life of love. Of course this love stemmed from her faith. But her response to this dereliction was to surround these dying people with love, that they might end their lives in dignity, not as the refuse of the earth, but as human beings valued, loved and cared for. The love of Mother Teresa has been communicated to the other women who joined her in the Sisters of Charity, whose communities throughout the world are beacons of love for the poor.

Blessed Charles de Foucauld (1858–1916). Although Charles de Foucauld, beatified in November 2005, lived several decades before the Second Vatican Council, his life embodied a different aspect of love to that of Mother Teresa. From 1901, he lived the life of a hermit in the African desert, and from 1905 in a remote area in the centre of the Sahara, surrounded by warring desert tribes. Charles de Foucauld understood his calling in terms of love. 'The Gospel shows me,' he wrote, 'that the first commandment is to love God with all one's heart, and that one must enfold everything in love.' His vision was to live a life of total love in the desert. First love of God, at the heart of which was the love of Jesus.

'When one loves, only one thing exists: the one who is loved. The rest of the world is as nothing, as non-existent.' So de Foucauld sought to live as Jesus lived and to live with Jesus. To live with Jesus meant especially silent prayer before the Blessed Sacrament, meditation on the Gospels and love for those people among whom he lived, especially the most poor. As a hermit, devoted to a life of prayer, Charles de Foucauld sought to preserve his solitude with Jesus, but it was said that he only allowed his solitude to be interrupted by the Touareg, the local tribe. While he did not draw any disciples to join him during his life-time (he was murdered in 1916), some years later a small group of French priests settled on the edge of the Sahara and founded a monastic community. The fruit of Brother Charles' love is seen especially in the Little Brothers of Jesus, now a world-wide congregation, living a simple life-style of work, service and prayer among the poorer strata of the population in the manner of de Foucauld.[1]

L'Arche and Jean Vanier. Another model of love is offered by the distinctive community life of L'Arche, founded by Jean Vanier (1928–). L'Arche began in 1964, when Jean Vanier, a French Canadian and son of a former Governor-General of Canada, lived for a time with two severely handicapped young men in a village in northern France. Out of this experience grew several convictions: that it was important for handicapped people to have normal relationships involving a real reciprocity, that handicapped people have much to give as well as to receive, that mixed communities of handicapped and normally active people could provide a framework for all to live as brothers and sisters, and so to give an example to a society more and more tempted to reduce relationships to what is functional or pleasurable. Although not all members of L'Arche are Christians, the inspiration is Christian, coming from the Gospels and especially from the Beatitudes.

Shaping a New Society

So far these examples are inspiring instances of exceptional Christians demonstrating a heroic degree of love in their lives. In three of these four instances, this heroic love has led to the foundation of a new family in the Church. But are there any examples of this love that comes from the Holy Spirit impacting the wider society and beginning to transform a whole culture?

An earlier chapter has identified solidarity as a key Catholic concept for the renewal of society and culture. The examples given of solidarity on a massive scale were all of one historic moment in the life of a nation (Philippines, Poland, South Africa, Ukraine). Almost inevitably these moments of action in solidarity did not last long after the hour of crisis. So we return to the question: are there any instances of renewed faith issuing in a new fellowship of love so strong as to begin to renew the life of a nation and its culture?

This transformation of society and culture has certainly been a goal of some of the new ecclesial movements, in particular the Focolari movement, Comunione e Liberazione and the Community of Sant' Egidio. The Focolari movement, with its spirituality of love expressed in communion, has sought in addition to smaller local communities to found miniature cities living the Focolari charism in several countries.[2] Chiara Lubich has developed the idea of an economics based on the idea of communion, which means business enterprises devoting their profits and focusing their energies along three lines: their own development, aid to the deprived, and supporting structures that form people in a culture of giving rather than receiving.

Pentecost 1998

In 1998, for the first time a Pope invited the new ecclesial movements and communities to join him in Rome at Pentecost to celebrate this feast of the Holy Spirit together. Greeting a vast crowd of 200,000 the Holy Father spoke of 'this wonderful event of ecclesial communion'. John Paul II continued: 'The Church expects from you "mature" fruits of communion and commitment'. The new movements are to insert their 'experiences into the local churches and parishes, ... always remaining in communion with the pastors and attentive to their indications.' The Pope refers to the 'criteria of ecclesiality' listed in the earlier document on the Laity, which includes 'an acknowledgment of a legitimate plurality of forms in the associations of the lay faithful in the Church and at the same time a willingness to work together'.[3]

The three movements that have responded strongly to the Pope's appeal are the Focolari, the Community of Sant' Egidio and the Catholic charismatic renewal. Since 1998, these three movements have made a deliberate effort to cooperate, and it has become common for them to invite speakers from the other two movements to their major conferences. Perhaps the high point of this collaboration to date was the New Europe ecumenical conference at Stuttgart in May 2004, when these three movements all played a major role.

What has this to do with love? First, a deeper communion is an expression of love. Second, it may be significant that the Focolari movement and the Community of Sant' Egidio are two movements that have particularly sought to develop new corporate expressions of Christian love and solidarity. And the Catholic charismatic renewal is probably the movement that has most strongly emphasized the need for attention and submission to the Holy Spirit.

A Particular Challenge

In new ecclesial movements and new communities, experiencing with enthusiasm the breath of new life coming from the charism of their founders, we almost always find that a great closeness develops between the members. In a first phase, there is much generosity of spirit with a deep level of personal sharing that impresses outsiders. New communities are often milieux where the New Testament words 'See how they love one another' have an evident application. However, there is often a tension between cultivating close fellowship in community and a real openness to serve and to welcome others outside the community. Outsiders can be experienced as a threat to the intensity of commitment of the community members. Outreach to others can be preoccupied with recruitment, with less interest being shown in those who have no recruitment potential. It is the struggle between exclusivity and serving the wider body.

It would seem that the communities most tempted in this way are those that are more middle class, educated and prosperous. The movements and communities giving a major priority to the poor are in much less danger, because their very commitment to the poor protects the purity and the disinterestedness of their love. This is true of such communities as L'Arche and Le Pain de Vie in France and a new order like the Missionaries of the Poor, founded by Fr Richard HoLung in Kingston, Jamaica.

It may be appropriate to end this reflection on love by citing some comments made in the 1930s by a Reformed pastor in France, Louis Dallière, who was faced with the differences between an authentic revival and a sect. Dallière made the following comparison:

> 1. A revival is a movement of the church and for the church; a sect is a movement outside the church and against the church. 2. A revival draws attention to the fundamental doctrines of the church; a sect organises itself around a particular point of doctrine. 3. A revival normally produces a current of love within Christianity; a sect does the opposite.[4]

This reflection is helpful today. The danger of sectarianism is not just found outside the Church. It is possible to have a spirit of sectarianism within the Catholic communion. Perhaps Dallière's most important insight concerns the centrality of love in authentic revival and renewal.

Notes

[1] The Little Brothers of Jesus were founded in 1956 by Fr René Voillaume (1905–2003), followed in 1963 by the Little Sisters, co-founded with Sr Madeleine of Jesus (1898 –1989).

[2] These include Italy, Switzerland, Germany, Brazil, Argentina, the Philippines and Cameroun.

[3] John Paul II, *Christifideles laici* (1988), para. 30.

[4] *D'Aplomb sur la Parole de Dieu*, pp. 8-9.

CHAPTER SEVENTEEN
Looking Forward in Joyful Hope

'May the God of hope fill you with all joy and peace in believing, so that by the power of the Holy Spirit you may abound in hope' (Rom. 15:13).

I have left hope until the last. It might have seemed more appropriate to follow the traditional order of the theological virtues, and to end with love, since 'faith, hope, love abide, these three; but the greatest of these is love' (1 Cor. 13:13). But hope speaks most strongly of the goal. Hope is our orientation to the fulfilment of God's plan. Hope gives direction. Hope expresses a vision. Paul says, 'we rejoice in our hope of sharing the glory of God' (Rom. 5:2). The hope of the Church is nothing less than 'sharing the glory of God'.

Individual Hope and Corporate Hope

The hope of which the New Testament speaks is a corporate hope, the hope of the People of God, the hope of the Church. The hope of 'sharing the glory of God' is not a private hope, but the hope of the whole Body of Christ. But if we ask how strong has this hope been in the Catholic Church of recent centuries, I think we have to admit that it has not been strong. The real hope of the Catholic people has been the salvation of their souls, that is, to go to heaven when they die, whether via purgatory or not. But this is not a corporate hope. This is an individual hope for my own future. Of course, we also hope for the salvation of our loved ones, but that does not of itself make this a corporate hope.

It is through our bodies that we belong to a corporate reality: a family, a tribe, a nation, a society. That is, it is through my body that I form part of a social body. The same applies to the Church at all levels. A hope that is just for the soul cannot be a corporate hope. Our corporate hope is possible only through the salvation of the body: through the resurrection of Jesus. His resurrection prepares the resurrection of our own bodies when he comes again in glory. That is why the noun-form 'salvation' in the New Testament refers to our final deliverance from all evil in the resurrection of the dead. So Paul writes, 'For God has not destined us for wrath, but to obtain salvation through our Lord Jesus Christ'

(1 Thess. 5:9). 'Therefore I endure everything for the sake of the elect, that they also may obtain salvation in Christ Jesus with its eternal glory' (2 Tim. 2:10).

The lack of a strong corporate hope is one of the most serious signs of spiritual weakness in the Church today. In many parts of the Church in the West, our numbers are declining. There are fewer people at Mass, fewer vocations to the priesthood and to the religious life, more churches that it is difficult to keep open, many scandals lowering the public reputation of the Church and of the clergy. In many ways, our dioceses are having to manage decline. This is not an encouraging task. It is true that not all the signs are discouraging. The decline in the number of priests can stimulate greater lay participation in the life of the Church. There are parts of the world where the number of priests is increasing. There are flourishing new movements and new communities, even in some of the nations with the worst signs of decline. But the deeper question remains: where do we look for our hope?

Restoration of the Hope of the Church

The recovery of the authentic hope of the Church is present in the documents of the Second Vatican Council, but it is much more fully developed in the *Catechism of the Catholic Church*. The hope of the coming of the Lord and of his Kingdom is present in the Constitution on the Liturgy, because all the sacraments foreshadow and prepare for the final completion. Thus,

> In the earthly liturgy we take part in a foretaste of that heavenly liturgy which is celebrated in the Holy City of Jerusalem towards which we journey as pilgrims...With all the warriors of the heavenly army we sing a hymn of glory to the Lord; venerating the memory of the saints, we hope for some part and fellowship with them; we eagerly await the Saviour, Our Lord Jesus Christ, until he our life shall appear and we too will appear with him in glory (SC, para. 8).

This hope was further spelled out in Chapter 7 of *Lumen gentium*, that deals with the 'Pilgrim Church' and the unity between the Church in glory, the Church suffering in the purification of purgatory and the Church militant on earth.

However, it is in the Catechism that the corporate hope of the Church is more clearly spelled out. It is here that the biblical renewal of the last century is showing its fruits in recapturing the eschatological thrust of biblical messianic faith. It is no accident that this recovery is linked with the new understanding of the covenant with the Jewish people. The Jewish people are by God's calling the bearers of the messianic hope. During the centuries when it was commonly believed that God had rejected the Jewish people, the corporate messianic hope of the Scriptures was still present in the Church and in her liturgy, but it was no longer directly sustained by the Jewish root. The recognition today that the Jews are still 'the people of the covenant' inevitably aids the recovery of the messianic hope of the Church. This fact is recognized in the Catechism in the heading above paragraph 673: 'The glorious advent of Christ, the hope of Israel'. This hope will then intensify as the Church progressively recovers her roots in Israel and manifests her authentic identity as the union of Jew and Gentile in one Body through the cross (cf. Eph. 2:15-16).

We should expect to find a rediscovery of the hope of the Church in those communities with a particular love for the Jewish people as the elect of God (this has nothing to do with partisan politics) and for their heritage. It can be seen, for example, in the Community of the Beatitudes, founded in France in 1974, and now present in many nations, including Israel. Their publications show how immersion in the Scriptures of Israel, freed from 'replacement' spectacles, opens up the Messianic hope of the whole Church.

Maybe one of the most practical ways of stimulating the 'blessed hope' is to teach the meaning of the *Our Father*. After all this most basic of all Christian prayers was given by the Lord to the disciples when they asked him how to pray. In this prayer, immediately after the acclamation of our heavenly Father, the second petition is 'Thy kingdom come'. The Catechism teaches us: 'This petition is "*Marana tha*," the cry of the Spirit and the Bride: "Come, Lord

Jesus'"(CCC, para. 2817). The next paragraph continues: 'In the Lord's prayer, "thy kingdom come" refers primarily to the final coming of the reign of God through Christ's return'(CCC, para. 2818). If the Christian people knew that this is what they are praying for, and if this is prayed deliberately and consciously, then how would it be possible for the Church not to recover her corporate hope?

Benedict XVI was elected Pope during the Year of the Eucharist. This year was preceded by the issue of the encyclical letter *Ecclesia de eucharistia* (2003). In this encyclical, John Paul II spoke of the 'eschatological thrust' of the Eucharist: 'The Eucharist is a straining towards the goal, a foretaste of the fullness of joy promised by Christ (cf. Jn 15:11); it is in some way the anticipation of heaven, the "pledge of future glory". In the Eucharist, everything speaks of confident waiting "in joyful hope for the coming of our Saviour, Jesus Christ"' (para. 18). But the Eucharist cannot play its full role in the renewal of the Catholic Church until the gospel of the Kingdom is clearly preached and the Eucharist is once again experienced as the anticipation of the glory to come with the Parousia of the Lord.

That is the scope or, as the French say, *l'enjeu* of church renewal.

Glossary

The following are abbreviations cited in the text:

AA	The Decree *Apostolicam actuositatem* of the Second Vatican Council (1995)
AG	The Decree *Ad gentes* of the Second Vatican Council (1995)
CA	Encyclical Letter *Centesimus annus* of Pope John Paul II (1991)
CCC	*Catechism of the Catholic Church* (1994)
DH	The Declaration *Dignitatis humanae* of the Second Vatican Council (1995)
DV	The Constitution *Dei verbum* of the Second Vatican Council (1965)
EN	The Apostolic Letter *Evangelii nuntiandi* of Pope Paul VI (1975)
ES	Encyclical Letter *Ecclesiam suam* of Paul V (1964)
FC	The Apostolic Exhortation *Familiaris consortio* of Pope John Paul II (1981)
FR	The Encyclical Letter *Fides et ratio* of Pope John Paul II (1998)
GDC	The *General Directory on Catechesis* of the Congregation for the Clergy (1997)
GS	The Constitution *Gaudium et spes* of the Second Vatican Council (1965)
IM	The Bull *Incarnationis mysterium* of Pope John Paul II (1998)
LG	The Constitution *Lumen gentium* of the Second Vatican Council (1964)

MND	The Apostolic Letter *Mane nobiscum domine* of Pope John Paul II (2004)
MR	The Report *Memoria et reconciliatio* of the International Theological Commission (1999).
NMI	The Apostolic Letter *Novo millennio ineunte* of Pope John Paul II (2001)
OT	The Decree *Optatam totius* of the Second Vatican Council (1965)
PP	Encyclical Letter *Populorum progressio* of Paul VI (1967)
RH	Encyclical Letter *Redemptor hominis* of Pope John Paul II (1979)
RM	Encyclical Letter *Redemptoris mater* of Pope John Paul II (1987)
SC	The Constitution *Sacrosanctum concilium* of the Second Vatican Council (1963)
SRS	Encyclical Letter *Sollicitudo rei socialis* of Pope John Paul II (1987)
TMA	The Apostolic Letter *Tertio millennio adveniente* of Pope John Paul II (1994).
UR	The Decree *Unitatis redintegratio* of the Second Vatican Council (1964)
UUS	Encyclical Letter *Ut unum sint* of Pope John Paul II (1995)
VS	Encyclical Letter *Veritatis splendor* of Pope John Paul II (1993)